The Successful Capital Campaign

From Planning to Victory Celebration

H. Gerald Quigg, Editor

Council for Advancement and Support of Education

© **1986 by the Council for Advancement and Support of Education**

ISBN 0-89964-248-9

Printed in the United States of America.

The Council for Advancement and Support of Education (CASE) provides books, art packages, microfiche, and focus issues of the monthly magazine, CURRENTS, for professionals in institutional advancement. The books cover topics in alumni administration, creative communications, fund raising, government relations, institutional relations, management, publications, and student recruitment. For a copy of the catalog "RESOURCES," write to the CASE Publications Order Department, 80 South Early Street, Alexandria, VA 22304.

Book design by Richard Rabil
Cover illustration by Michael David Brown

Council for Advancement and Support of Education
Suite 400, 11 Dupont Circle, Washington, DC 20036

Contents

Figures

Introduction

The capital campaign is a subject—or, rather, a way of life—to which an institution's president, development officer, and trustees must devote a great deal of time and attention. Those of us who make our living in development have seen the capital campaign change significantly over the years, becoming more and more frequent and with larger and larger goals.

The Successful Capital Campaign: From Planning to Victory Celebration presents a comprehensive and in-depth look at this important area of fund raising. CASE and the many authors who have contributed chapters join me in hoping that the volume will fill a need in these three areas:

• **Education:** This book provides an encyclopedia on the capital campaign. Seasoned professionals and newcomers alike can use it as a resource.

• **Technical assistance:** This book provides a directory for fund-raising professionals and key volunteers who need technical information on the many aspects of the capital campaign.

• **A record:** The book records in one document all aspects of current thinking on the capital campaign. This record of the experience and thinking of some of the finest professionals in the field will be an invaluable tool to all associated with philanthropy.

The men and women who have contributed to this volume have all directed one or more capital campaigns. What they offer goes beyond theory to include what they have learned through experience. Also, except for Royster Hedgepeth who wrote Chapter 21 on the public university perspective, all of the authors represent the private sector. Since my own career has been in the private area of the nonprofit sector and since that is where the capital campaign originated, the book has a private-sector thrust.

I am honored to have been asked to edit this important publication for CASE. Not only is the task rewarding, but it is another way to be meaningfully involved in a professional organization that has contributed much to my own personal and career growth and is a significant and influential force in philanthropy today. Having known CASE since it evolved from the American Alumni Council and the American College Public Relations Association in 1974, I am delighted with the organization's current strength and breadth of service. And I believe that this book will be an important addition to CASE's publications.

H. Gerald Quigg
Vice President for University Relations, University of Richmond

Chapter 1

What Is a Capital Campaign in Today's World?

H. Gerald Quigg
Vice President for University Relations
University of Richmond

When I first entered the fund-raising profession, my boss referred me to Harold J. Seymour's book, *Designs for Fund-Raising* (New York: McGraw-Hill, 1966), as *the* text to start to learn the business. At this time—the early '60s—the capital campaign was only an occasional event on campus. It was a special project involving an intensified effort to produce a specific dollar amount in a short time, often with outside counsel providing direction. It was also periodic. The president, staff, and volunteers geared up for an intense effort and, when it was over, returned to the routine of the annual fund and alumni events. This doesn't mean that the pressure wasn't on or that development people were less knowledgeable or that the campaign itself wasn't vital to the institution. It's just that we were not constantly "in the fast lane" as we are today.

The campaign of the early '60s differed from that of the '80s in four basic ways:

1. It was an occasional event. Every five years or so, the institution would gear itself up for a massive effort.

2. It had a specific pledge period, usually three years. While many institutions continued the annual fund during the capital campaign, others dropped it. This was a mistake as they soon discovered.

3. Most capital campaigns were directed toward bricks-and-mortar projects. These were the golden years for higher education, and trustees, faculties, and presidents built with abandon.

4. Outside counsel often provided campaign direction since many development officers lacked in-depth experience. The capital campaign was a real event, and, for the most part, the campus community found it exciting and challenging.

As the golden years ended and the pressure of needs became greater, the educational community moved into more sophisticated long-range planning. This incorporated the entire package of institutional needs into a plan that was widely shared with all constituencies. Comprehensive long-range development programs included operating, capital, and endowment needs over a five- to 10-year period. Goals were larger than ever. The case statement became a marketing piece printed in grand style and giving an overview of the needs. When institutions found that 10-year plans became obsolete too soon, they switched to five-year plans.

This comprehensive development program paved the way for what I call the comprehensive *intensified* development program of today. It is characterized by:

- incredible dollar goals;
- continuous or extended time periods;
- sophisticated marketing efforts; and
- well-trained professional staff.

To the astonishment of many, institutions are achieving ever higher campaign goals. For example, Stanford, Harvard, and Princeton have goals in the high nine-figure range. We expect leadership institutions with great potential to have large goals, but even smaller institutions with seemingly less potential are setting their sights high. Some of these may be letting trustee or presidential egos influence goals—someone says, "If old Siwash can raise $100 million, so can we."

Campaigns seem to go on forever and often are extended when the goal is achieved. Further, campaigns come closer and closer together. At the University of Richmond, we successfully completed a $50-million campaign, and within a year and a half we were beginning another for $55 million.

The methods and technology of campaigning today are very sophisticated: They include extensive prospect research, computer tracking, word processing, and telemarketing. Development staff people are highly qualified and bring to the campaign expertise in computer technology as well as in the tried and true campaign methods. Fund-raising counsel must compete with on-campus development people who are experts at the capital campaign. This is a dramatic change from just a few years ago.

When I called this first chapter "What Is a Capital Campaign in Today's World?" I intended to provide a definition of what will follow. But I must admit that, while fund raising may be more precise, sophisticated, and technical than it used to be, it is still not an exact science. Fund raising deals with people, and people are not easy to define.

When I was in the Army, I was always told that no matter how sophisticated weaponry became, nothing could ever replace the foot soldier. The same can be said of fund raising; no matter how good our support services become, nothing replaces the person. Fund raising must still depend on the person-to-person contact of a good solicitor seeking a gift from a potential donor.

Today, just as in the past, capital campaigns rely heavily upon volunteers who are committed to the cause, motivated to make personal contacts, and directed by staff people to carry out their mission with enthusiasm. Goals may grow larger and the campaign more frequent, but it is still the individual who makes the difference between success and failure.

Chapter 2

What Are the Values and Purposes of a Capital Campaign?

Edward G. Coll, Jr.
President
Alfred University

C hoosing to conduct a capital campaign is perhaps the most important de-cision a campus administrator can make. The decision commits trustees, senior administrators, deans, faculty, and staff to thousands of hours of ad-ditional work. It exposes the institution's admitted weaknesses and opens up for public scrutiny its self-proclaimed strengths. This is a decision that should be made only after an in-depth study of the institution and its situation, and only if every-one involved has a strong conviction of the value of the cause.

Every ambitious organization wants to improve itself. To do this usually requires large sums of money that are ordinarily not available in operating budgets. The capital campaign is the quickest and most efficient method of creating new dol-lars to address the needs both of ambition and of survival. These new dollars create new programs, facilities, and endowments for the future security of an institution. Colleges, universities, and independent schools that have been willing to invest the time, energy, and planning required for a capital campaign have reaped their reward, not only in dollars but in other bonuses as well. This chapter focuses on the values of the capital campaign—in addition to its dollar goals—and on what it can do for the institution.

The case statement

We would all agree that discussing the merits and strengths of our institutions is easy. Campus leaders love to describe their institution's accomplishments, past and present, to all who will listen. But that won't suffice when you are asking people to contribute to a capital campaign.

The basic ingredient of any capital campaign is the case statement. This official document lists the needs of the institution as well as the arguments, analyses, and comparisons that support the appeal. To create the case statement, the institution must examine and articulate its mission and designate the priorities established to reach its goals. The process requires an introspective review that should be as thorough and exhausting as the 10-year reaccreditation process.

The case statement as an educational tool

Educating the institution's constituency is a never-ending task. To do this, most institutions use the annual report, periodic issues of the student newspaper, and the alumni publication. Each of these presents the state of the institution in a particular form. The case statement provides a new weapon in the information arsenal. Properly prepared and marketed, the case statement is an influential educational tool that spells out in detail a new and challenging thrust for the institution—a thrust that projects ambition, energy, and a renewed sense of professional development. It alerts readers to the challenges ahead and mobilizes the institution's family in support of the goals.

The case statement is the most important document in the capital campaign. Its preparation and content should not be treated lightly, for it must bear both the presidential imprint and the strong endorsement of the campus community.

Leadership

While money is the primary focus of capital campaign efforts, other benefits emerge during the campaign. Leadership is the major new resource.

An institution cannot initiate a successful capital campaign without adequate public leadership to champion its cause. As part of the planning process, administrators evaluate the campaign organization chart and the availability of proven leadership to fill the slots.

An organized capital campaign challenges the institution's existing leadership and provides a testing ground for potential new leaders, who display their talents in the execution of their campaign responsibilities. The new leadership discovered in this way often has a greater value to the institution than the dollars raised. Long after the money is spent, these leaders will continue to contribute their efforts to the institution. This campaign bonus cannot be measured by the short-term financial goals of the campaign.

Old friends and new supporters

It's an axiom in institutional fund raising that previous donors are the best source of new funds. These donors have already invested in the institution and, through their gifts, have become better acquainted with it and its leadership. If the institution used previous gifts prudently, these donors usually respond promptly to a personal appeal for a capital campaign.

But a campaign truly challenging to the institution reaches new donors for a sizable portion of the goal. One of the fundamental objectives of any capital campaign should be to identify and cultivate new donor groups. Every institution must work constantly to increase its donor pool, thereby enhancing its funding opportunities and replacing previous donors who, for a variety of different reasons, have stopped contributing.

The capital campaign is the best vehicle for donor expansion. High dollar goals force leadership to expand the quest for donors and to develop a new cadre of individuals, corporations, foundations, and organizations who will provide vital long-term support.

Organizing and executing a program to cultivate new support sources may be tedious and difficult, but it must be done. Institutions that ignore new donor cultivation will face a catastrophe in the long term. People who know nothing about an institution will usually give just as much as those who dislike it—that is nothing. Keep this admonition in mind and consider your capital campaign as an opportunity to raise friends as well as money. Institutions and organizations that raise new friends raise new money too.

The annual fund vs. the capital campaign

In the '50s and '60s, a debate brewed over what should happen to the annual fund during a capital campaign. Established older institutions and the Ivy League schools stood firm on their decision to run both campaigns simultaneously. Purists pointed to churches and synagogues that routinely organized capital projects while continuing to emphasize weekly contributions. Newer participants in capital fund raising suspended the annual fund, fearing the reaction of alumni and friends to multiple appeals.

The debate has been more or less resolved. In recent years, America has accepted the need of nonprofit institutions to build and expand while they continue to sustain a viable annual operations budget for day-to-day needs.

If your institution is embarking on a capital effort, don't worry about the impact on the annual fund. To the contrary, you should look to the future. Devise methods to sustain the involvement of your new capital donors by soliciting them for the annual fund on completion of each capital gift or pledge. In this way, your capital campaign can enhance the annual fund long after you've reached your goal.

An instrument of morale

Although a capital campaign takes great effort and usually leaves participants exhausted, its successful conclusion creates a sense of accomplishment and pride within the institution that is difficult to match. The marshaling of leadership in pursuit of lofty campaign goals, the joys and frustrations at the ups and downs of the project—these add excitement to the routine of institutional life.

A successful campaign is always perceived as an institutional effort that involves every constituency, and everyone shares in its success. Alumni can take pride in the diversity of the donors who, with their gifts, acknowledge the institution's prestige and enduring value. Faculty can see it as an endorsement of their teaching and research skills and the staff as public approval of their efforts to bring the institution to new levels of distinction and public service. The capital campaign is the cohesive agent that binds together the best attributes of the institution and those individuals who make it function.

Chapter 3

The Long-range Planning Process

William L. Pickett
President
Saint John Fisher College

T his chapter discusses the ways in which institutional long-range planning relates to successful capital campaigning. While a sense of strategic direction is essential to the effective organization of an institution, long-range planning rarely becomes a priority until a major institutional decision or undertaking is imminent. Thus for many colleges, universities, and independent schools, the point at which the need for long-range planning becomes clear is when a capital campaign is under consideration.

A capital campaign is a major effort to focus the energies and resources of all those associated with the institution. The focus is on the future, specifically on those aspects of the institutional future that will determine the fundamental direction and tone of the institution and that typically require major increases in human and financial resources. Long-range planning is the process by which the institution seeks to focus its attention on these issues.

This chapter defines long-range planning and discusses the participants, reviews a workable format for planning, and describes three general procedures.

A definition

Long-range planning is an organized effort to identify institutional priorities over at least a five-year horizon and to ensure that the behavior, both of the organiza-

---

Pickett was formerly the vice president for university relations at the University of San Diego.

tion and of its individual members, reflects those priorities. We can separate this definition into four important parts.

1. Long-range planning must be an *organized effort*. You cannot do it quickly and without thought. It is an important organizational activity that requires the attention of important institutional leadership throughout several levels of the organization. It requires resources, especially the professional staff who must guide and manage the process. It cannot succeed without the serious interest of the chief executive officer.

2. Long-range planning must cover *at least a five-year planning horizon*. Many institutions claim to have 10-year plans but these are usually five-year plans with a five-year extension. Planning for a shorter period than five years doesn't require the organization to take a full look at all aspects of the operation. The institution tends to focus attention on tactical changes to cope with current problems rather than developing strategies for the future.

3. Long-range planning seeks *to identify institutional priorities*. The essence of planning is choice. Planning enables an institution to move in one direction rather than in another. An organization that plans effectively will choose not to do most things in order to do a few things. Effective planning should eliminate institutional ambiguity about mission, goals, objectives, and operational decisions.

4. Long-range planning must ultimately result in *shaping institutional and individual member behavior*. This is especially important in academic organizations. Institutional priorities mean little unless they determine or at least influence the actual behavior of the organization and its members. A long-range plan that "sits on the shelf" is not only a waste of resources, both financial and human. It also conveys to the members of the organization just how unimportant long-range planning really is to the institution's leaders. Often, when long-range planning is ignored in this way, it is because the people who should implement the plan were not involved in the planning process. Long-range planning will not work unless academic officers and faculty leaders are involved in the process of developing the plan and its priorities.

The participants

Advancement administrators should be involved in the long-range planning process, but only to the same extent as other key administrators. The institutional community needs to see the planning effort as an institutional process, not as something the development office needs in order to raise money. Long-range planning seeks to identify real priorities, important to the future of the institution, not just those for which there may be a philanthropic market.

Long-range planning should involve both internal and external participants. Internal participants should reflect the important internal constituencies whose commitment to the plan will determine its ultimate effectiveness—faculty, students, administrators, trustees, and the president.

In academic organizations, the faculty are the ultimate decision makers. In institutions where the most important activity is teachers teaching and students learning, the decisions of individual faculty members have the most powerful impact on the quality and the success of that endeavor. Faculty members must be at the center of the long-range planning process. It's not enough to include the formal academic leadership (academic vice presidents and deans); influential members of the faculty should be involved, including leaders of both tenured faculty and junior faculty.

Involving students in the process can be a problem. Serious planning efforts often last longer than an academic year, making it difficult to include the same students throughout the process. And it's not easy to find students who have the time, the perspective, and the communication skills to function effectively in a group that includes the leadership of the institution. But long-range planning needs students who can express the concerns and viewpoint of those who are the clients of the educational process. The managers of the planning process should take extra care to ensure that this important input is made effectively.

Administrators are not only important as participants and decision makers in the life of the institution, but they are the people who have gathered and analyzed internal and external information essential to long-range planning. It's particularly important to include administrators whose jobs bring them into direct contact with the external environment. These include staff in public relations, fund raising, admissions, continuing education, and so on.

Trustees play a dual role in colleges, universities, and independent schools. They are part of both worlds—the outside world and the world inside the institution. They must be effectively represented in the internal dynamics of an institution's long-range planning.

The president has a singularly important role in the process of long-range planning. He or she must provide strong leadership to the overall planning process by making it clear that the discussion and conclusions of the planning group will be taken seriously. In addition, however, the president must also be an advocate for his or her own view of the institution and its future. The president's vantage point is unique, and no one else can as effectively represent the needs and desires of the entire institution. While the president's view should not be the determining one, it should be advanced strongly and reasonably. The other participants in the process need to hear the thoughts and concerns of the chief executive officer.

In addition to the internal participants in the planning process, important external constituencies should also be involved. External constituencies are often the source of resources needed to implement the priorities identified in the planning process. These constituencies include:

- alumni;
- parents of current students;
- parents of past students;
- nonalumni, nonparent friends;
- foundation executives and trustees;
- corporation executives;
- business people;

- leaders of educational institutions from which students come;
- leaders of educational institutions to which students go;
- members of institutional advisory councils;
- members of the board of trustees; and
- opinion makers, especially those in the media.

These participants represent a great diversity of viewpoints and opinions from which the planners must develop a synthesis. The synthesis should represent the valid viewpoints of institutional members while at the same time presenting alternatives for future actions. The board of trustees is the usual setting for the approval of such a synthesis, and it is usually the president who provides the leadership to create a consensus.

Long-range planning must involve those people who will determine the ultimate success of the plan. At the same time, the planning process cannot be held hostage to a multiplicity of interests and actors. The chief executive officer must guide the process and ensure that both participation and action are the result.

Format for long-range planning

The details of the long-range planning effort reflect the nature of the educational institution, the environment in which it functions, the history of institutional planning, and the personalities of the participants. As a result, there is no recipe for successful long-range planning. Many different models exist, and each will work for some institutions but not for others. The details are not important as long as the planning effort addresses these five essential questions:

1. Where are we?
2. How did we get here?
3. Where are we going?
4. Where do we want to go?
5. How do we get there?

These questions, which are not as simple as they may seem at first glance, must be answered fully and honestly.

Where are we?

The fundamental issue in most long-range planning efforts is not what the future will be or should be but rather what the present is. The present for any organization is not static; as an institution's environment changes, and new problems and situations develop, the people within the institution must modify and adapt their behavior. It is very hard to pin down exactly what the present is at any given moment because it is always in a state of change. Long-range planners must reach a consensus on the present before they can address the future. For example, some of the faculty may see the college as a classical liberal arts institution while others believe it to be a vocationally oriented institution. Until this basic difference in perception is articulated and resolved, discussions of the future will reflect this continuing disagreement. Planners must reach a consensus on four important aspects of the institution's present: (1) The basic mission of the institution must be articulated and approved by a workable portion of the organizational community; (2) its present operating characteristics must be identified, measured, and communicated; (3) the institution's strengths and (4) its weaknesses must be evaluated in terms of programs, students, faculty, administration, facilities, and finances.

How did we get here?

Once the planners have agreed on what the present is, they must understand how the present came to be. They must assess the history of the institution. The present did not "just happen" but rather reflects the confluence of organizational, environmental, and personal issues. Every institution has a certain momentum of which the present is the concrete expression. An understanding of that momentum is crucial to an understanding of the organizational forces that have created the present and can build the future. Planners must examine the institution's history, especially its recent history. Identifying both continuities and discontinuities in the institution's history can help planners identify those forces that are strongly linked to fundamental values and mission and those that are merely pragmatic expressions of institutional adaptation.

Where are we going?

This question addresses the "default option"—if the forces currently driving the institution continue without change, where will the institution go? Given the present and the past out of which it grew, what does the future look like? The planners should describe this future in terms of the institutional mission and the specific operating characteristics listed above. The planning group needs to evaluate the default option future and assess its appropriateness for the institution.

Where do we want to go?

The planning group needs to determine exactly how the future course of the institution should differ from the default future in terms of mission and goals, operating characteristics, and specific accomplishments or programs. Planners should describe this future as specifically as possible in order to provide guidance for decisions about future resource allocation. Unfortunately, this stage is where all too many planning efforts *begin*. But you cannot deal with the future until you have fully understood the present.

How do we get there?

Now that the planners have a clear idea of where they are and where they want to be, they can describe the resources that will be needed to create the desired future. At this point, you might think of the institution as a rocket. The rocket already has momentum provided by resources expended in the past; this momentum will determine the course the rocket will take. If you want to change your institution's course, you must provide additional resources. This additional energy is often small compared to the total energy expended, but if it is appropriately applied, it can significantly change the direction and mission of the institution, just as it would that of the rocket.

Long-range planning procedures

Which type of planning effort will be successful for your institution? Three basic options are available to institutional leaders. First, they can use decision-making channels, groups, and procedures already in place. Existing cabinets, councils, and committees can often do successful long-range planning if all important constituencies are represented and if the institution is not facing any especially critical threats now or in the foreseeable future.

Second, leaders can create low-profile groups and structures to facilitate planning. These groups involve representatives of all important constituencies but conduct long-range planning as they would any other institutional business. Finally, leaders can establish a high-profile group for planning. The establishment of such a high-profile group indicates the importance of long-range planning to the life of the college, university, or independent school.

Conclusion

Long-range planning is an important part of the successful management of an academic organization. It is a prerequisite for a successful, major fund-raising effort because it forms the basis of the campaign's case statement. The case statement is important not only because it identifies the pressing needs of the institution but because it communicates the sense of institutional direction essential to fund-raising success. In a fundamental sense, then, the major benefit of long-range planning is that it forces members of the academic community to be clear about who they are and what they do. The articulation of this understanding will give them the sense of purpose and mission that will focus their efforts and increase their effectiveness.

Chapter 4

Before the Campaign Begins: An Internal Audit

D. Chris Withers
Associate Vice President for Development
University of Richmond

A successful capital campaign doesn't happen overnight. It takes years of planning, clearly defined priorities, and carefully and conscientiously coordinated volunteers and staff. Just as we would not drive across the United States without a map, neither should we seek the approval of our board of trustees for a major capital campaign without a well-documented case and campaign plan. It is important to be able to articulate the difference between the planning for a campaign and its implementation.

Further, it is an axiom in development that what happens *before* a campaign begins is far more important than conducting the campaign itself. It is also our job, on occasion, to slow down the over-eager volunteer or the new president who is anxious to please his or her trustees by getting the "big one" or making a quick, early "score."

Several years ago, a colleague and I were asked to consult with a political candidate for statewide office. He had announced his intention to run less than six months before the primary and wanted to catch up in a hurry. His intentions were good but he wasn't interested in planning; he needed cash *now*. At meeting after meeting he would say, "Let's just solicit 'em all—now!"

Similarly, a novice at this game might say, "If you divide the amount needed by the number of names in the prospect pool, you'll know how much to ask each person for; if we want to raise $1 million, let's ask 1,000 people to give $1,000 each—that's not a lot."

It's our job as development professionals to slow these people down and to make sure that all of the work that should precede the campaign gets done.

This chapter concentrates on seven areas of preparation for the capital campaign:

1. the plan itself;
2. institutional endorsement;
3. the role of the president;
4. internal readiness;
5. external readiness;
6. the top 100; and
7. a successful annual fund.

The plan itself

In the United States and throughout the world, higher education is regarded as an activity in the public interest. However, only the U.S. regards development and public relations as functions necessary to colleges and universities. Thus, institutional advancement is really an American creation.

Most foreign institutions are owned and managed by the government, no tuitions are charged, and admission tends to be highly selective. In the United States, the federal government plays a limited and decreasing role in higher education. Involvement is generally through state government. As a result of this limited government involvement, colleges and universities must compete for resources. This is what I like to call the "mission" of institutional advancement and the capital campaign: To enable each institution to advance in a competitive environment and to acquire—or attempt to acquire—the resources necessary to support its many programs.

In this era of economic uncertainty, financial support for institutions is of paramount importance. The means by which our institutions obtain this financial support is largely contingent upon leadership, both internal and external. The president, executive staff, deans, faculty, and so on, compose internal leadership. External leadership comes from trustees, alumni, and friends. This highly valuable group of external leaders contributes time, energy, and gifts. They are the key to success of the entire public relations, institutional advancement, and capital campaign operation. Institutional advancement must make a continued effort to maintain and strengthen their loyalty and support.

The first comprehensive capital campaign began at Northwestern University in the 1920s. Research indicates that even then campaigners first put on paper ideas and concepts about goals, needs, and methods. At the University of Richmond we have a saying: "If you can't write it, you can't do it." Each of the development officers must write a detailed fund-raising plan for his or her unit for the year. We also did this for both of our major ($50 million and $55 million) capital campaigns.

Chapter 13 deals with the campaign plan in detail, but here are some of the points that a capital campaign plan should include:

• An introductory paragraph such as the following:

This plan has been written to provide a basis of common understanding among members of the Board of Trustees, the volunteer corps, and the development staff who will be working on the campaign. It is possible that strategy, schedule, budgeting, etc., may change during the next five years as progress and problems occur. Should that happen, it is important that changes be decided as conscientious departures from an approved plan and not simply as expedient adjustments to temporary conditions. The needs for additional staffing and budget increases are derived from the campaign strategy and schedule.

- a description of terms, needs, and length of the campaign;
- what gifts count toward the goal;
- table of organization for the campaign;
- scale of gifts;
- division unit and collective number and dollar goals;
- methods;
- campaign calendar, strategy, and schedule;
- budget;
- promotional literature; and
- staffing and support services.

Institutional experience may vary but I think we can all agree on the importance of starting early. If you have an important Founders' Day celebration coming up two or three years hence or a key institutional date several years away, it is not too early to begin planning now.

Institutional endorsement

Some say, "You can't very well encourage others to eat in your restaurant if you don't eat there yourself." It is important to have early unanimity of purpose and understanding from internal constituencies. Often you can achieve this by holding a campus-wide retreat for faculty and student leaders, administrators, and the board of trustees. You will find that this works best if you actually go off campus and focus on the issues themselves. The trustees must take over ownership of the campaign, and for this you must get these busy people away from their offices and homes so they can concentrate on the campaign. Retreats can be very successful in galvanizing interest, responsibilities, and leadership gifts. Such a retreat, or "campaign symposium," should serve as the culmination of the planning meetings involving deans, faculty, and administrative leadership.

The role of the president

The president is the principal spokesperson for the university, the campaign needs, and the program. He or she is *the* principal solicitor of the largest gifts. Very few significant gifts will occur without his or her involvement. But be careful to use the president's time wisely; determine the level of gift requiring his or her involvement and use other volunteers for gifts below that level. Even if you are scrupulous about this, the president must anticipate spending a significant (50 percent) portion of time soliciting and cultivating major gifts throughout the entire campaign.

In a successful capital campaign, the president has at least six specific roles.

1. The president is fully aware of the central role of trustees in fund raising. He or she understands the board, knows its problems, and has the support of his or her chief aides in creating assertive board leadership in fund raising.

2. The president works hard to enunciate the master plan of the institution and to obtain a consensus on mission and goals.

3. The president uses his or her time and appearances wisely; if he or she were to be involved in every fund-raising operation, appearing before every group that requested a speaker, there would be no time for the truly important events.

4. The president should meet regularly with senior development staff to assess campaign strategy and analyze strengths and weaknesses.

5. The president must be willing to spend considerable time cultivating prospects for major gifts.

6. The president should insist on continuity in development strategy rather than zigzagging from one approach to another. Successful capital campaigning is continuous, not episodic, and patient steady effort is more productive than pushing for the "fast buck."

In his recent book, *Mega Gifts*, Jerald Panas lists several reasons why donors make major gifts. The most important reason is "belief in the mission of the institution" (Chicago: Pluribus Press, 1984, p. 227). The president must personify the character and the mission of the institution that he or she leads. Remember: People give to people. Confidence in the chief executive is often the deciding factor in the big gift.

An institution takes on the style of its chief executive. Many presidents are comfortable with early morning breakfast meetings; some like one-on-one solicitations rather than presentations to large groups. Whatever your president's style, he or she should exemplify the character, the hopes, and the mission of your institution.

People give to institutions whose representatives articulate goals clearly and project solidarity and confidence. How successfully your institution's president does this can determine the success or failure of your capital campaign.

Gonser Gerber Tinker Stuhr, in their 1977 publication on public relations in development, stressed the importance of the president's primary responsibility for fund raising: "No matter what other valuable contribution the president makes to the quality of the institution he or she serves, attracting a brilliant faculty and an able student body, encouraging academic innovations, ensuring prudent management of the resources of the institution, and all the rest of it, [the president] will have failed if [he or she] does not provide for the institution's financial need" (*On Development*. Chicago: 1977, p. 72). The president must be primarily responsible for and active in any successful fund-raising campaign.

I knew our campaign at the University of Richmond would succeed when I heard President Heilman tell the faculty, shortly after the launching of our first capital campaign, "You won't be seeing very much of me for the next several years. I'm going to be out on the hustings raising money for your salary and funding the needs that you helped develop."

Internal readiness

Faculty members, committees, administrators, and all the deans from various campuses will be eager to submit detailed lists outlining their needs. It will take important trade-offs and considerable discussion to pare the list down to a goal that is reasonable but will still meet these needs.

You should also consider the following questions:

1. Do you really know your constituency? Do you have adequate information about their backgrounds, where they live, where they work, their hobbies, interests, giving potential?

2. Are you properly staffed? Does each staff member have a clearly defined job description and area of concentration? Do staff members know the "big picture" as well as their own individual goals, methods, and so forth?

3. Have you considered the budget needed to complete the campaign over the three- to five-year period? (General guidelines range from 7 to 12 percent of the capital campaign goal.)

4. Have you done an equipment inventory including word-processing and information retrieval capabilities and the basics such as where you will assemble kits, stuff envelopes, prepare worker packets? Do you have tables, chairs, working areas? People's "space" tends to be exceedingly important and unless support staff and professional staff alike have some input into the planning for this item, you may face problems of declining morale. For example, during an intense phase of our campaign, we had to move administrative offices from one building to another. This led to concerns about security, confidentiality, and loss of records, in addition to the "down time" involved in the move.

5. What about campaign materials? Have you done an inventory of pledge cards, business reply envelopes, kit folders, materials on memorial opportunities, tax information, workers' kits, question-and-answer folders, fact brochures, transmittal forms, master and division report cards, and audio-visuals? Have you researched your institution's impact on the community—culturally, religiously, socially, and through its athletic programs?

6. Have you thoroughly reviewed your gift recording and acknowledgement system? The best way to do this is to "walk" a gift through the various steps, from opening the envelope to completing the respective transmittals for on-line data entry, batching, communicating with the business office about gift turnaround time, and finally sending out the gift receipt and acknowledgement letter as well as any other additional letters you may wish to send (particularly to those who send a new or increased gift). Have you determined who will acknowledge gifts—the campaign chair, the staff, or the president? Do you have a tickler system for billing?

7. What kinds of donor recognition do you have, and what levels of gifts are they for? Do you have the vehicle in place for memorial gift opportunities, naming gift opportunities for buildings, scholarships, professorships, chairs? Are you prepared to deal with the variety of vendors who supply plaques, scrolls, citations, proclamations, and portraits?

Staff and institutional advancement *cannot* function as an adjunct to the rest of the campus enterprise but only as an integral part of it. Once you have obtained the financial resources the institution needs, you must continue to be involved with how those resources are used so you can report to the donors how their gifts have undergirded and strengthened your institution's educational mission.

External readiness

Successful fund-raising campaigns are composed of many elements. In a recent issue of *Philanthropic Digest* ("Why Fund-Raising Programs Succeed," May 1985, p. 12), George A. Brakeley, Jr., chairman of Brakeley, John Price Jones Inc., listed the following elements:

- a valid case, forcefully stated;
- strong leadership;
- fields of support;
- careful timing;
- a combination of proven strategies and innovative procedures;
- favorable working conditions and an adequate budget to do the job; and
- preprogram planning.

Brakeley includes institutional image in preprogram planning. You must understand your institutional image so that, in your campaign, you can market your institutional strengths and strengthen your institutional weaknesses. How well is your institution regarded by the constituent group? By your community? Is a public relations program needed in particular areas?

During the course of two major capital campaigns at the University of Richmond, we tested the market in several ways:

1. We did a feasibility study involving 50 to 100 key people. In our study—unlike that described in Chapter 6 of this volume—we did not employ outside counsel but rather sought to answer the questions asked and to develop a marketing strategy based on what we learned.

2. We conducted what we called a "raters' program," whereby we identified a larger pool of influential people in a wider geographical distribution and asked for their confidential comments about prospects, capacities, institutional strengths and weaknesses, and the institutional image in general.

Polling of public opinion is important before you announce the campaign. What form the poll will take and how extensive it will be depend on the role of research in your previous development efforts and how well you know your various constituencies. Do you have a sophisticated major gift tracking program? It is one thing to know who your leadership gift prospects are; it's another to know how they view your institution and your campaign. You need to have this information *before* you ask them for their support.

How well do you know your institution's fund-raising history? Has there been concern and involvement over the years among the various constituent groups—parents, alumni, and neighbors? Will additional cultivation be needed before you can seek the large gifts? What is your relationship with the media? Institutional presidents are often reluctant to take a stand in controversial situations and reply "no comment" when members of the media call. Some say they have been burned too many times—their remarks have been misquoted or distorted. Has your president done this often enough to annoy or antagonize the media? If so, you need to know this and be prepared to deal with it during the campaign.

In our various annual fund campaigns at the University of Richmond, we often test-market a particular direct-mail package to a particular audience or at a particular time of the year—perhaps we do all three or a combination of them. This can help you judge the potential for success of your capital campaign. Take your case statement, table of needs, campaign goal, and projected gift pattern to others. Ask constituent leadership whether they are realistic.

Involving your constituency can be a complicated and time-consuming project, but it also can and should be simple. As Harold Seymour said, the best public relations "is the sum total of an almost infinite number of tremendous trifles" (*Designs for Fund-Raising*. New York: McGraw-Hill, 1966, p. 163). You can encourage your external publics to identify with your institution through the persistent application of the procedures listed below.

- Seek their advice and opinions.
- Promote meaningful visitation.
- Ask them to join something at your institution.
- Quote them and make sure the quote gets adequate visibility.
- Ask them to make a speech.
- Seek their testimony.
- Use their names.
- Take their pictures.
- Send advance proofs.
- Pay attention.

But whatever you do, do it *sincerely*.

Now you have written the campaign plan and identified the case, you have obtained campus-wide institutional endorsement, you have made sure the president understands his or her role, you have analyzed your office's strengths and weaknesses and determined that you are ready for the campaign, and you have test-marketed the case and needs to the external pressure groups. The next task is to compile a list of names of those prospects who will make or break your campaign.

The top 100

We used to say, you get 80 percent of the money from 20 percent of the donors. These days it's 90 percent from 10 percent. For this reason it is vital to broaden your base of support. Those $100, $500, and $1,000 donors to this campaign will be the $10,000, $25,000, and $50,000 donors to the next one. But for the campaign you are planning now, you need to assess the capacity and readiness of the top 100 donors. You start by reviewing your entire VIP file, your corporate and foundation file, as well as files for law firms, vendors, alumni and parents, and the board of trustees and adjunct advisory board.

We used to believe in "the rule of thirds"—one gift equivalent to approximately 10 percent of the campaign goal added to the nine next highest gifts would equal approximately one-third of the campaign goal. The next 90 gifts would equal the second third of the campaign goal. All other gifts would equal the bottom third. If this were true, it would mean that the top 100 gifts account for between 65 and 70 percent of the entire campaign. Recent studies, however, indicate that the rule of thirds, while definitely true for larger campaign goals, does not apply to campaigns of less than $1 million. In smaller campaigns, the top 100 gifts make up only about 45 to 50 percent of the total.

Whether your campaign is large or small, you should use prospect research to compile an annotated list of the top 100 prospects. For each prospect, you will need to know the gift range to be asked for, the key solicitor, the purpose for which the gift will be sought, and how long it will take to bring the prospect to a state of readiness to receive the proposal.

At the University of Richmond all of our development staff are required to list their top 100 prospects annually for their respective campaigns (law school, business school, etc.). We review the names of these prospects on a monthly basis for tracking and cultivation moves to see how we can bring the prospect closer to making a gift.

Remember, your job as chief development officer is major gifts, major gifts, major gifts! You should constantly track the top 100 prospects but be flexible—revise the list if you need to as the campaign progresses.

A successful annual fund

Now we come to the stickiest wicket of them all—the role of the annual fund in a capital campaign.

The role of a capital campaign is to maximize dollars during an intensive period of time. The annual fund should broaden the base and identify donors who can move up to the capital campaign level of giving. How do you maintain both these development efforts and see that each fulfills its role?

Whatever strategy you use, Rule No. 1 is: *Keep your annual fund going throughout the capital campaign.* In most institutions, annual giving provides basic budgetary support. Annual fund donors who qualify for donor recognition clubs become the basis for your major gift prospects in subsequent capital campaigns.

As G. Steven Wilkerson and Adrienne W. Schuette comment in *Handbook for Educational Fund Raising* (Francis C. Pray, editor, San Francisco: Jossey-Bass, 1981, pp. 33-34), "The 'double ask' may be too complicated and confusing for many." They suggest, "If you have a good annual giving program, you keep it going and count it toward the capital campaign goal. Inform the constituency about current and long-term needs. If you can't have a good annual giving program at the start of the campaign, make its development integral to the latter stages of the campaign so it is well launched to run beyond the end of the capital effort." They continue:

Special gift clubs, recognition programs and personal solicitations for annual giving are prime opportunities to discuss deferred gift options. At least once a year, direct-mail appeals can mention information available to those who wish to plan their giving more carefully. Successful exploitation of annual giving for deferred gifts depends on communications between deferred giving, the capital giving and the annual giving staffs. A part of the evaluation of a development staff must be based on its members' ability to break loose from territorial concerns to strengthen the impact of the other officers responsible for other constituencies.

On the other hand, if your programs are *not* sophisticated and your annual fund is *not* well established, you may find that the double ask is appropriate. Then you might ask your donors either to designate a portion of their total campaign commitment for the annual fund or to be willing to receive a separate solicitation at a later date from the annual fund leadership and staff.

In areas where we've conducted specific regional campaigns, we have concentrated on the major gift prospects for the capital campaign. We've asked everyone else to consider making their "largest annual gift ever" to the annual fund.

Several years ago I heard Gary Evans (now vice chancellor for development and university relations at the University of North Carolina at Chapel Hill) give a talk on this particular topic. He reviewed three options: (1) Absorb the annual fund into the capital campaign; (2) Conduct a double ask; or (3) Conduct a separate ask.

• *Absorb the annual fund.* This option provides only a single solicitation, a more clearly focused case, and less confusion. At the same time you increase the base of support for the annual fund. There are three disadvantages to this strategy: You lose the unique distinction of the annual fund, there is no special annual fund presentation, and you stand a chance of securing a lower gift.

• *Use the double ask.* The advantages of the double ask include a personalized capital *and* annual fund appeal, a more efficient use of volunteers, and elimination of the "hard sell." There are two disadvantages to this option: Donors find it hard to appreciate the distinction between the two appeals, and you may find it difficult to train workers.

• *Use the separate ask.* Using the separate ask gives you the advantage of a clear distinction between annual and capital campaigns; volunteer training is much easier; and there is more emphasis on the annual fund. But you may run into donor resentment over the second request; you will have to use many more volunteers and shift from annual to capital.

Which strategy you use and how clearly you articulate the strategy to your constituents through campaign newsletters, alumni magazine, and campaign literature comprise one of the most important ingredients in determining campaign success. Whatever method you use should prevent overlapping solicitations and confusion among constituencies.

Conclusion

Capital campaigns are complex and intense. Each one is unique and has strategies special to the particular institution. During an Olympic year, an institution launched its capital campaign with all the sparkle and ballyhoo of a political convention, including balloons and an Olympic torch. That approach would repel a group of Philadelphia attorneys planning a campaign to endow a scholarship fund. Clearly, mechanics and methods differ according to the situation. As unique and complex as capital campaigns may be, however, they are still the best means of galvanizing donors and volunteers to reach a worthwhile goal for a clearly documented set of needs within a specific period of time.

So, do your precampaign tasks carefully. What you do *before* you launch the campaign may well be more important than any single event during the campaign and may make the difference between attaining that ambitious goal and missing it altogether.

Chapter 5

Fund-raising Consultants

H. Sargent Whittier, Jr.
Vice President for Development
St. Lawrence University

A consultant is the person who borrows your watch to tell you the time.

C onsultants come in for more than their share of jokes these days. Yet anyone who has worked on a capital campaign with a good consultant comes
away from the experience with a very high regard for the profession.
There are some situations in which outside counsel may not be necessary. In
my experience, those are few and generally occur when the staff is so professional
and experienced and so large that it can provide the benefits of outside counsel
"in house." Few institutions have that luxury, and many of those that do choose
to use counsel anyway. They prefer to take advantage of a consultant's ability to
enrich the discussion of strategy and to give the institution the benefit of an outside perspective.

What a consultant can do

The good consultant uses analytical skills and insight gained through experience.
He or she helps those involved with the campaign debate the issues and plan the
most effective tactics and strategy. The consultant suggests issues that might otherwise be overlooked and advises about all aspects of the design and execution of
the campaign.

A consultant also provides an outside point of view, one that is unbiased and
unemotional. Most of the people closest to an institution know it only by its parts.
We can compare their situation to that of several blind people trying to describe

an elephant from an examination of one part. It's hard to see the whole picture when we are closely associated with one particular aspect of the institution. The skilled outside observer brings a perspective that is invaluable. The consultant helps us to see ourselves more clearly and gives us the benefit of his or her experiences with a variety of other institutions.

In almost all cases, counseling firms can provide some services that an institution is hard-pressed to provide for itself. Often consultants are better at providing an objective assessment of the readiness of the constituency and the commitment of potential leaders. They can help build and develop a staff. General management issues frequently affect an institution's ability to raise funds, and some consultants are skilled at helping institutions address these issues. The development of a case for the campaign is an area where consultants are particularly useful. People closest to an institution tend to simplify the case—"We are worthy and therefore others should help." Outside counsel can help an institution focus a case on the factors that will make it more compelling to prospects who are at a greater physical or emotional distance.

Consultants can also stimulate consideration of issues beyond fund raising that will have a bearing on the productivity of a campaign. Sometimes, in dealing with such broader issues, consultants become involved in areas beyond their specific expertise. This is not a problem as long as all concerned recognize the situation and weigh the advice accordingly.

Often counsel can play an important role with a president or school head who is new to the post or is not experienced in fund raising. The consultant can help the chief executive consider his or her role in the management and execution of a program and can assist in evaluation, formulation of plans, development of appropriate staff levels, and budgeting.

In the same vein, do not overlook the useful role that counsel can play with junior members of the staff. A good consultant can assist in their professional development and training. As they plan and execute programs, younger staff members may benefit greatly from time spent reviewing issues or techniques with a skilled outsider. The details of those programs may be less familiar to senior people, yet may affect overall success of the campaign. Such exposure to counsel can also heighten the staff member's sense of self-worth and importance.

Types of consultants

In the early days of the profession, consultants raised money for organizations not equipped to do so for themselves, but today's consultants provide a far broader array of services. They work as individual practitioners or in firms that range from two or three people to 40 or more, and the variation in services offered is just as great. We can identify three general categories of consultants: larger fund-raising firms, purely consulting firms, and individual practitioners.

Firms with large staffs can provide consulting as well as actual campaign staffing and on-site direction. These firms tend to provide many different services to many kinds of clients in addition to education. They may serve hospitals, YMCAs and YWCAs, churches, and community service agencies. They tend to operate on a retainer or flat fee basis. Some of them provide additional services such as writing or prospect research.

The purely consulting firms confine their practice to consulting over a range of issues, working with the institution's staff. They often limit their practice to education or to a few other types of cultural organizations and some health care clients.

The individual practitioner offers the same kind of consulting but on a more limited scale. This consultant usually operates within a narrower range, serving the kind of client with which he or she has had the most experience. Some consultants specialize in particular areas such as planned giving.

Defining your needs

Many different counseling relationships are possible, and your job is to seek and develop a relationship that serves the needs of your institution and the challenges it faces at this particular time. Every situation has special characteristics that call for tailored responses. If your institution has no history of effective fund raising, or has no experienced staff, or is considering a campaign significantly larger than any undertaken before, you may need a fairly intensive consulting relationship that includes a full study of the organization and regular visits and meetings. Counsel might assist in developing and training the staff, educating the board, or advising the president or school head.

If your institution has a more successful track record and an experienced staff, you may need counsel to do an assessment in the beginning and maintain a less intense ongoing relationship for the rest of the campaign. Such assessments are useful from time to time, particularly at the start of a consulting agreement, for they provide an objective view of institutional status and give the consulting firm an in-depth understanding of the institution and the forces and attitudes present. If your institution's trustees, leadership, staff, and history are all strong in fund raising, you might want a consultant on a quarterly or semiannual basis to provide an external perspective and to aid in regular assessment, monitoring of progress, and refinement of tactics.

An effective counseling relationship takes real effort. Much of that effort should come well before you select the consultant. Careful self-analysis will clarify the purposes counsel might serve. These purposes will vary with the strengths and weaknesses of the institution and the stage at which it finds itself.

Selling the idea

Once you have determined that you need a consultant's help, you must convince trustees and other leaders. This may not be easy. They have hired an experienced development officer and probably do not want to spend more money on a consultant. There is no easy formula to persuade them of your need. Consultants are increasingly common in both business and higher education. People who have had good experience with them will be more supportive than those who have not. You may want to point out that your institution has a competent financial officer, but employs an outside firm to manage endowment investments and retains auditors to monitor operations. Your institution may also have had experience hiring outside designers or publications experts for the production of important admission or fund-raising pieces.

In a sense, hiring a consultant is one way of buying insurance; you have the confidence that an impartial outsider is monitoring the progress of your campaign efforts. The level of internal expertise should determine, at least in part, how much you use counsel and how much it will cost. The better the staff and the stronger the history, the less money you will need to spend on outside counsel. In the end, it is the institution's own people who must raise the funds. Consultants are not a substitute for competent staff, but should supplement internal leadership.

Choosing a consultant

The choice of counsel ought to be based on thorough internal discussion of your institution's particular needs. Often interviews with potential consultants will help you identify the needs, clarify your options, and focus on the critical issues. Candor and realism are essential. Involve both the people and constituencies who might obstruct a successful program as well as those who will work for its success. If your colleagues feel that they influenced the selection and the role of counsel, they are likely to have a positive outlook and be willing to cooperate.

But in the end, those who are most centrally involved and will have the greatest contact with the consultant should be the ones to make the final decision. For instance, if counsel is to work closely with trustees, key members of the board must support the idea, be involved in developing the role, and participate in the choice. If counsel will work primarily with the president, head, or development officer, then that person should play the primary role in the decision.

Pay attention to questions of professional ethics. Be wary of firms that promise results or claim to have a magic formula. Consultants cannot assure access to funding sources, nor do they have the key to the vault of any prospects. If they offer to give you inside information about individual prospects, they may sell *your* inside information to the next client. Reputable firms make no such promises.

Reputable firms also recognize a possible conflict of interest. A firm working with similar institutions or with other institutions in the same geographic area does not necessarily have a conflict, but it is a good idea to discuss the question just to be sure. The kinds of firms you want to do business with live on their good reputations and are careful to avoid questionable situations.

The final choice ought to be made on two levels: the general strength, expertise, and appropriateness of the firm, and the qualifications and "fit" of the individual or individuals to be assigned to the client. Interviews with and presentations by the firms you are considering will provide a basis for comparison. Be certain that you meet not only those who market the firm's services but also those who will actually do the work.

At this interview stage, do not expect the consultant to offer solutions and recommendations; in fact, beware of them. A good consultant takes time for an in-depth familiarization with the institution, its history, and its people before reaching conclusions and suggesting courses of action. Recognize that this is important and provide access and assistance. The quality of counsel you receive will be far higher.

In judging a consultant, look beyond the superficial. Don't let a consultant's age and how many campaigns he or she has worked on be the prime determinant. It's more important to consider the consultant's ability to define issues and to assess strengths and weaknesses of the institution as they relate to the issues. Analytical skills are as important as length of experience. What you need most is someone who can look at your institution and its opportunities objectively and assist you in evaluating options. This is also a "people business," and to be effective a consultant should be a person of strength in this area and in communication.

When you select a firm, you should talk to former and current clients. Don't hesitate to ask pointed and probing questions. Ask for a complete list of clients and do reference checks at various levels. For instance, a member of your board may know a key person on the board of one of the consultant's clients or your president or school head may be able to talk to the president of an institution that has used the firm. These checks provide a more complete view and are reassuring to those who will be involved with the consultant.

You can assess the "fit" of the individual assigned to your institution by face-to-face meetings. Both parties should feel comfortable with the relationship, including the key people with whom the consultant will be interacting. This is especially important if a firm representative will be placed on-site or will be directing the campaign. If the "chemistry" doesn't work, the relationship won't either. A poor match is a disservice to everyone, and most firms will be understanding and cooperative in ensuring that the relationship is a productive one.

When to involve counsel

Don't make the common mistake of bringing in a counseling firm when the campaign is ready to be launched. If you need a consultant then, you probably needed him or her earlier. Consultants report that they are often asked to do a feasibility study as the first step in the relationship. This reflects a misunderstanding of the consultant's role. Counsel can be far more valuable at an earlier stage. The decision to do a feasibility study should follow a full discussion of many campaign planning issues. You do not decide to do a feasibility study the day after someone concludes that funds are needed. Counsel should be involved in the discussion of strategy, only one element of which is whether to do a feasibility study. The best consultants provide much more than feasibility studies; they are most productive when they are partners in the planning of overall strategy as well as in the development of specific tactics.

Consultants can also help an institution develop campaign objectives and accomplish the other early steps that precede a campaign. Often, a consultant's advice at that time can help you avoid problems later on.

While some call in consultants too late, others dispense with their services too early. Often the consulting relationship is terminated as soon as the goal is in sight. But rarely has all been done that can be done to maximize results. Consultants can help you capitalize on your success and lay the groundwork for continuing effective fund raising. Often, the most difficult planning takes place at the end of the campaign, and outside counsel can be very helpful.

The world, however, is not always an ideal place, and your campaign may be well along before circumstances suggest that outside counsel might be useful. Progress might be slow and achievement of goals in doubt. Or there may be great success that suggests you might be able to achieve more than you originally hoped. At such a time, you might consider beginning a counseling relationship *in medias res*. Counsel could study the campaign and recommend ways to regain momentum or to enhance achievement. Or you might use counsel at the end of a campaign to audit its results and to assist in planning programs that extend its benefits, promote sustained giving, and prepare for future campaigns.

The amount of counseling attention you need may vary with different stages of the campaign. You won't necessarily need to sustain a high level of intensity throughout the entire campaign. When budgeting for counsel, consider varying the amount of help you get in order to extend the relationship over a longer period of time. I don't mean to suggest that counseling should be a permanent feature of any development program. For some institutions it is, although this often involves only the sharing of reports and a visit once or twice a year to keep counsel up-to-date for the next campaign.

Working with consultants

The consulting relationship should not be painless. If the consultants are doing their job well, they will ask hard questions and cause discomfort; they will force you to address issues you don't want to deal with; they will urge you to establish deadlines and timetables and then remind you about them; they will recommend that you consider strategies that test your will; and they will not be satisfied with easy answers. This is part of their value and it makes them critical to the success of any campaign. Outside consultants are not unsympathetic, but they are realistic. Consultants should often make you feel good about what you are doing, but just as often, if they earn their fee, they should make you squirm and they should challenge you to greater effort.

Counseling is most productive when egos are repressed. A defensive client is less likely to be well served. The consultant's fee is earned by probing and analyzing. The client who welcomes this gets his or her money's worth.

When you establish a relationship with fund-raising counsel, it is important to begin with a clear understanding of mutually agreed-upon services, expected outcomes, and costs. Try to minimize surprises. If counsel charges extra fees for certain services, you need to know.

As the relationship progresses, you and the consultant should reassess it together from time to time. Circumstances and issues change, and you may find that you need a different level or kind of counseling attention, or even a change in personnel. Different members of the counseling firm have different strengths and expertise. The firm may need to bring in another person when the situation changes and calls for different skills and talents. Educating a board of trustees is quite a different matter from invigorating an annual fund or developing the case for specific endowment objectives. All of these are areas in which counsel can assist, but different individuals may be best suited for the different tasks. The more open your relationship with the consulting firm, the more effective it will be. You need to be able to tell the consultant when it is time to make a change.

Fees

All reputable consulting firms and individuals charge set fees. Beware of the consultant who suggests that the fee be based on a percentage of the funds sought or raised. Most firms do not consider this appropriate or professional. The structure of fees will vary with the services performed, the people involved, and the nature of the firm, but all fees should be related to the actual time the consultant spends serving the client.

You will probably need to pay the consultant's out-of-pocket and travel expenses, and you should estimate these with the consultant at the start so you won't be unpleasantly surprised when the bill comes in.

Many firms change an annual retainer or flat fee that provides for a certain level of consulting services. Charges for specific services beyond these are billed in addition. The basic retainer may, for instance, provide for one or two days per month of the consultant's time. If the institution needs increased counseling or a study, the costs will increase. Some firms charge a fee based upon time actually spent on behalf of a client, and this may vary from month to month. Other firms combine both of these approaches.

I would be wary of a firm that proposed a specific package of services and fees without first assessing the institution's situation. The fees and proposed services should be tailored to the institution's circumstances. Don't hesitate to compare the proposed fees to those of other firms or to discuss them with the consultant's current or past clients.

Conclusion

If you choose to hire counsel, do it carefully and be certain that you have confidence in the person or persons with whom you will work. View it as a partnership, not an adversarial relationship. Don't waste the time you spend with the consultant. Be prepared for each meeting and make it productive. Expect your consultant to do the same. Set agendas, involve key people, and demand full attention and value. Don't accept everything your consultant says as gospel. Examine every suggestion and debate alternatives. In the end, you and your institution must make the decisions and be responsible for them.

If you feel that, because of the size of your campaign or the strength of your staff, you don't need counsel, you can still get some of the benefits. You can talk to colleagues, attend workshops, or even invite one-time visits or evaluations by peers. None of these will give you the advantages of an ongoing association with a consultant, but they do serve a purpose.

Consultants are no smarter than institutional leadership. However, the better ones are skilled at analysis and at isolation and identification of issues, and their wisdom is based on experience as well as an unbiased perspective. They are not infallible. If they appear to walk on water, it is only because they know where some of the rocks are.

Chapter 6

Testing the Market: The Feasibility Study

Richard Page Allen
Vice President for College Relations
Gettysburg College

D on't confuse action with progess in that period of time before the public announcement of a capital campaign. People who have worked in annual giving and capital area campaigns know that a certain amount of activity is necessary to yield fund-raising results. But in the preannouncement phase of a capital campaign, the reverse can be true—action taken too early can actually reduce your chances of reaching your goal.

Between 80 to 90 percent of the money received in your capital program will come from between 5 to 15 percent of your donors. Hence, it is absolutely essential that your leadership gift prospects be completely familiar with the campaign purposes and be ready to make the largest gift they can. How close these gifts come to the donors' full capability will determine how close you come to your announced goal. In other words, if a donor would give $3 million if he or she were fully committed to the campaign but will only give you $500,000 if solicited at this time, you should spend more time cultivating and involving that donor.

The feasibility study is a market survey that tells you how close your key volunteers and prospects are to full commitment. Unless they are fully informed, fully involved, and fully committed, they will not make their best effort for the upcoming capital campaign.

You may think that you already have this information about your key constituents because of your ongoing involvement with them. But administrative officers are often so close to the situation that they cannot judge objectively the extent to which volunteers and prospects *are* fully informed about and committed to institutional goals.

The feasibility study involves individual, confidential interviews with 20 to 50 key people or organizations. The information collected gives you an overall picture of the readiness of the people interviewed to support the proposed capital campaign effort.

If you are planning a feasibility study, the first decision to make is who will do it. You must determine who will conduct the interviews, who will correlate the results, and who will make the report to the institution. You have several options: You can use existing institution staff, newly hired campaign personnel, outside consultants, or some combination of staff and consultants.

Some organizations and a few consultants suggest that the interviews offer a significant cultivation opportunity and, for this reason, the staff should do them. In this way, staff members get first-hand information and can form their own conclusions instead of accepting them from "outsiders." Through the interviewing process, they will gain a real sense of what the constituents are saying about the campaign and the institution.

Others—and they are in the majority—believe that most college staff people cannot elicit honest and full responses to the important questions in the feasibility study interviews. Some also believe institutional staff are so close to the campaign project that they may hear only what they want to hear, overlooking or misinterpreting information provided by the prospects.

You should make a careful analysis before you decide to conduct your own feasibility study or to hire consultants. You may want to try a combination of efforts by consultant and staff. If you assign prospects for interview carefully and discuss and analyze the results with the consultant, you may find this method yields the best information and insights.

On the other hand, you may want to use outside consultants if you are in doubt about the institution's goal or the readiness of the constituency. The president and development staff may be criticized either for being too ambitious in their fundraising goals or for not being ambitious enough. It can be an uncomfortable position for the chief advancement officer who has to tell other key administrators and campaign leaders that the goal is too high or that the institution is not ready for a campaign at this time. But an outside consultant who conveys this news may be performing his or her most valuable service for the campaign.

You should develop an agenda for each interview in accordance with the institution's specific circumstances. Issues to be explored should include the prospect's understanding of the plans for the growth and enhancement of the institution and its services and how the proposed campaign will help attain these goals. The interviewer should ask questions to evaluate the prospect's level of confidence in the president and satisfaction with key volunteer leaders and board members. It's important to draw out the prospect about his or her feelings and ambitions for the institution.

You can begin the campaign cultivation process during the feasibility study by giving prospects a draft of the case statement before the interview. Their comments can be invaluable—not only in helping you develop the case statement itself but, more importantly, in indicating their level of understanding of the campaign and its purposes.

Last—and perhaps most important—the interviewer should ask what the prospect thinks will be his or her level of financial commitment to the upcoming campaign. Do not accept this amount as the gift to ask for when solicitation occurs. Instead, consider this perceived level of commitment as an indication of how close the prospect is to readiness for solicitation for the maximum gift you know he or she is capable of giving.

At Gettysburg College, we rate each of our leadership prospects on his or her total gift potential—if they were fully committed to the institution—and then assign a probability factor for reaching that potential if solicitation were to occur soon. For example, research, staff evaluations, and field evaluations have determined that Mrs. W has the potential to make a gift of $1 million over the next three years if she is fully committed to the institution and its campaign goals. But at this time, our best guesstimate is that solicitation would yield only 50 percent of that potential. We determined that Mr. C could make a gift of $100,000, and because he recently had some positive experiences at the institution, we gave his chance of making the full gift if solicitation occurred now a 90 percent probability. Finally, although Mr. and Mrs. G have the ability to make a $3 million gift to the campaign, their son recently had a bad experience with the institution, lowering to 1 percent the probability of their making that gift if solicitation occurs now.

When you make this type of gift potential and probability analysis on a case-by-case basis, you can make informed decisions about the institution's overall fund-raising potential. You can determine the timing of specific cultivation moves and solicitations and when to make the public announcement of a campaign goal.

When both potential and probability are high, you should schedule solicitation as soon as possible. But if potential is high and probability is low, you need to assign additional cultivation activities. If the probability is around 50 percent, your decision is not as clear-cut.

You can keep ratings for leadership prospects in a hand file or easily put them onto a spreadsheet on a personal computer. If you update this information regularly, at any given moment you can tell the chief executive officer or key volunteer leaders the fund-raising potential of your identified prospect pool. To estimate the results if solicitation were to occur within 60 days, you simply multiply the probability for each prospect by his or her potential. For example, we estimate the gift of Mrs. W, who has a $1 million potential and a 50 percent probability, to be $500,000. Add the estimates for each prospect in your pool to get an estimate for overall fund-raising potential at this time. At Gettysburg College we've been using this method since 1978, and we find that it predicts with great accuracy the overall outcome of our solicitation activities.

The feasibility study will produce information to help you assign probability ratings. The study and the resulting ratings can guide you in important campaign management decisions. If you compare individually projected gift results with the scale of gifts for your proposed campaign, you will see whether the proposed goal is too high, too low, or just about right.

Make sure that the feasibility study and the precampaign discussions are conducted on a confidential basis. During this time you are testing projected goals against available financial resources to determine what you can hope to accomplish in your campaign. You don't want to go public until you're ready.

The cost of a feasibility study varies widely depending on whether you use outside consultants and how much, as well as what types of costs are charged to the study. If staff members conduct the interviews and charge only their travel expenses, the costs are minimal. On the other hand, it can be quite expensive if outside consultants conduct the interviews and if most of the costs of doing the prospect-by-prospect analysis of the leadership pool are charged to the feasibility study. In 1985, feasibility studies costing anywhere from $15,000 to $50,000 were not uncommon.

The important decision about the use of outside consultants must be made in time for the feasibility study—if not earlier. If you decide to use an outside consultant for the feasibility study, you should involve that person or organization in the process as soon as plans start to unfold for the campaign. Most institutions can benefit from the use of outside consultants throughout their entire campaign process. The extent to which consultants work on your campaign—and the corresponding costs—will vary with the level of experience of your staff. Some organizations need full-time resident campaign directors while others prosper with periodic consulting on a weekly, monthly, quarterly, or even semiannual basis. You should look for a consultant who will help your institution determine the amount of consulting needed and adjust that service and the fee accordingly. (See Chapter 5 for more about choosing and using consultants.)

At the conclusion of the feasibility study, key volunteers and the administrative leaders must decide how to proceed. The level of readiness of your prospects may make it clear that it would be ill-advised to start on a campaign now. Instead, you need to undertake an extensive program of cultivation and targeted solicitation for a period of six to 18 months. In other circumstances, you may decide that your institution's need for the resources is so urgent that even though the constituents are not at a high level of readiness, you need whatever funds you can raise in the near future, and therefore the campaign should go forward. Whatever you decide, the feasibility study will show you how to organize the goals, volunteers, and staff in order to maximize potential and results.

The results of the feasibility study often show that the campaign goal should be less than had been hoped because some major prospects are not yet fully informed and committed. In this case, it may be best for key volunteer leaders to select a preliminary confidential goal and then proceed with a combination of solicitation and cultivation events. After the solicitation and cultivation, the leaders can reconsider the preliminary goal in light of the results to date, and lower or raise the goal before making a public announcement.

An underlying rule of any fund-raising campaign is that it must be successful. People like winning teams. Failure to meet campaign goals will reduce enthusiasm for the institution.

For this reason, it's best to announce your campaign only after careful analysis of the results of initial solicitation, the feasibility study recommendations, and the best guesstimates of the potential for the remainder of your pool. Remember, you can always raise the goal if certain key prospects come in at gift levels higher than originally anticipated.

The feasibility study and the data prepared for the analysis of the prospect pool should prevent your institution from confusing action with progress. The feasibility study and its implementation should help you run a campaign that will bring you the highest level of fund-raising success possible.

Chapter 7

Prospect Research

Jan L. Grieff
Manager of Development Research
University of Pennsylvania

Your fund-raising effort won't be successful without research. Good research provides you with a pool of prospects who are able and willing to give to your institution. The research process that produces this prospect pool takes place in three stages: prospect identification, Level 1 research, and Level 2 research.

Prospect identification

Prospect identification should be an ongoing process at your institution, whether or not you have a researcher on your staff. (If you do not have a researcher and are considering a capital campaign, I urge you to hire someone quickly.) The first step in planning your campaign is to review your prospect pool to determine the total donative potential. This dollar figure will assist you in determining both a realistic goal and the priorities of the campaign. Once you have established the goal, you should develop a gift table.

In any special gift program or capital campaign, you need a gift table to show the total dollar figure and the number of gifts necessary at each gift level. In addition you need another table to illustrate the breakdown by constituency at each gift level. These tables not only give you a graphic picture of what you will need to make your campaign a success, but also provide direction for the research staff during the prospect identification phase.

Figures 1 and 2 are gift tables for a $10-million capital campaign. Figure 1, illustrating the number of gifts necessary at various gift levels, directs the research staff

37

during the prospect identification phase. The research staff must identify and perform Level 1 research on 1,134 "suspects." In addition, 567 of the suspects will become prospects and require Level 2 research.

Figure 1 also demonstrates the need for a pool of volunteer leaders to solicit these prospects. If you use one solicitor for every four prospects, you will need to identify and research approximately 150 key volunteers.

Gift amount	Number of gifts		Number of prospects	Number of suspects
$ 1,000,000	3		9	18
$ 500,000	6		18	36
$ 100,000	12		36	72
$ 50,000	24		72	144
$ 25,000	48		144	288
$ 5,000	96		288	576
Total	189		567	1,134

Figure 1: Gift Table for $10-million Campaign

Figure 2 provides an analysis of gifts by gift level and constituency group. According to these figures, research should spend approximately 80 percent of the time on identifying individual suspects and 20 percent on identifying corporate and foundation suspects.

Gift amount	Number of gifts	Number of prospects/suspects by constituent group		
		Individual	Corporate	Foundation
$1,000,000	3	6/12	0/0	3/6
$ 500,000	6	12/24	3/6	3/6
$ 100,000	12	21/42	6/12	9/18
$ 50,000	24	45/90	15/30	12/24
$ 25,000	48	120/240	12/24	12/24
$ 5,000	96	255/510	24/48	9/18
Total	189	459/918	60/120	48/96

Figure 2: Gift Table by Constituency

These gift tables provide direction to the research staff regarding the number of suspects required for the success of your campaign.

Because the research staff cannot review your total constituency, you will need a strategy to break it down into a more manageable size. Figure 3 lists the types of potential suspects most likely to become prospects. For example, previous donors are more likely to give than people who have never given.

In order to identify suspects who fit one or more of these criteria, you will need to use a variety of sources including internal records, printed materials, and screening programs (both personal and electronic).

Individuals	Corporations	Foundations
Previous donors	Previous donors	Previous donors
Giving society members	Giving society members	Trustee-affiliated foundations
Trustees	Trustee-affiliated corporations	Local foundations
Former trustees	Vendors	Foundations with similar interests
Alumni	Major corporations with subsidiaries in your area	
Parents	Companies that use your institution's placement services	
Faculty/staff	Local independent businesses	
Prominent families in your local area		
Relatives or descendants of families memorialized by your institution		
Descendants of early founders of your institution		

Figure 3: Potential Capital Campaign Suspects

Internal records such as giving histories, alumni questionnaires, purchasing records, and lists of former trustees will be useful. Even a closer look at the names of some of the facilities on your campus might turn up some potential suspects.

External sources such as local corporate and foundation directories will help you identify potential organizational suspects, as well as individual suspects and potential volunteer leaders. Remember, it is individuals who make the decisions in organizations. A good source for finding prominent alumni of your institution is *Who's Who in America, College Alumni Directory*.

Screening sessions can serve as cultivation events as well as identifying suspects. You might assemble a group of alumni to assess the giving potential of other alumni. At the University of Pennsylvania, our screening sessions have been conducted regionally and by profession (accountants screen accountants, lawyers screen lawyers, and so on).

Many development officers believe that those involved in development research have internal, rather than external, responsibilities. I believe that the research staff should function in an external development role, particularly with regard to screening sessions. Researchers know best what questions need to be addressed when prospects are being screened. For example, a person not involved in prospect research might assume a prospect's giving potential is high because "she drives a Mercedes" or "his wife wore a diamond tiara" or "they take expensive vacations." But these facts indicate how a person spends his or her money, not how much he or she actually has.

Several companies perform electronic screening for nonprofit organizations. According to their advertisements, these electronic screening programs combine demographics and computer technology for efficient identification of the highest potential prospects. The electronic screening process uses real estate values, income estimates, high-ticket merchandise purchases, educational status, and other publicly available information to pinpoint prospects. In addition, the programs use recent census data, including Standard Metropolitan Statistical Area codes, to evaluate prospects.

An electronic screening service can be very useful but it should augment your own screening programs, rather than replace them. Its best use is to provide a list of suspects. For example, an institution with a large constituency may use electronic screening to focus its personal screening program.

For smaller organizations, an electronic screening program can be expensive. One consulting firm, for example, charges $11,000 to screen up to 15,000 people. If this screening program were able to replace the manual research function, it would be cost effective, but as it can only augment existing screening programs, most small institutions cannot afford it.

Level 1 research

After you have identified the suspects in your constituency, you will need to conduct preliminary Level 1 research. This research determines whether the suspect becomes a prospect. Figure 4 lists the elements necessary for Level 1 research for each segment of the constituency. Most of the basic information for this level can be found in internal sources.

The development officer and the research staff must keep in constant communication during both prospect identification and the preliminary research phase. You should establish a schedule for the number of suspects to be identified in a given period of time. You will also need to hold regular meetings of the development staff to move suspects to prospect status.

At the University of Pennsylvania, we use several methods to promote suspects into prospects, including committee review, staff visits, and screening sessions. A committee of development officers and a member of the research staff meets peri-

Individuals	Corporations	Foundations
Giving history	Giving history	Giving history
Name	Name	Name
Home address	Address	Address
Business address	Local subsidiary address	Giving interests
Business title	Officers/directors	Officers/directors
Family ties to your institution	Giving interests	
School/year (if alumni)	Number of alumni employed	
	Number of recruiting visits	

Figure 4: Level 1 Research Elements

odically to discuss suspects ready to become prospects. Often development officers have pertinent information about suspects that would never be revealed except through discussion. Sometimes this information eliminates a suspect rather than moving him or her into the prospect pool. For example, the suspect has four children attending college and has little disposable income, or is already overcommitted because of major gifts to another organization; the foundation is undergoing a change in its giving purposes and now is the wrong time to ask for a gift. These are all key reasons why a suspect may never make it into the prospect pool or at least not at the gift level originally hoped.

Development research is not an exact science, and often only a visit to the suspect can determine whether he or she has prospect status. For example, researchers may be unable to determine the exact donative potential from existing sources. In the case of a former donor or volunteer leader who has lost touch with your institution, only a visit can determine whether his or her interest in your institution can be reestablished.

Screening sessions may help you determine the prospect status of a group of suspects. Peer review enables you to assign gift ratings to individual prospects or to delete them from the list. Again, the purpose of a screening session is twofold: It provides you with sound direction in assigning gift ratings and it can be used as an opportunity to cultivate.

Level 2 research

Review sessions, personal contact, and screening should enable you to determine your prospect list. At this point, you are ready for Level 2 research. Level 2 research should give you enough information to "know" the prospect and to determine financial worth and donative potential to the greatest extent possible.

Figure 5 on the next page lists the elements necessary for Level 2 research for each constituency. Notice that the information accumulated in Level 1 research forms the basis for Level 2 research.

As you read this list of elements, you will see that development research is a time-consuming process. Although the three lists of elements are just about equal in size, you will find it much easier to research a corporation or a foundation than to research an individual.

When you are planning your campaign, be sure to include the time you will need to conduct the required research. An average that I use to determine the productivity of the research staff at the University of Pennsylvania is to figure one day to do Level 2 research on each prospect. In reality it can take as little as two hours to research a corporation or foundation, but it may take up to a week to research an individual.

Using this average, you can figure that it will take approximately 717 days (or approximately three years) to perform complete research on the 567 prospects for the $10-million campaign in Figure 1. And that's only for Level 2 research; it does not include the identification phase or Level 1 research. For a more exact estimate of the time needed for all three phases of research, you should multiply this figure by one and one-half. This gives you four and a half years.

Of course, we are assuming that only one person does the research. If your research office is well-established and has been engaged in ongoing prospect identification, one researcher may be enough. But it is more likely that you will have to add to your present staff for the duration of the campaign.

And don't forget that information obtained at the beginning of a five-year campaign will be out-of-date by the end. Research should not be a "once and done" process, but an ongoing one. Someone in the research department should be responsible for keeping individual and organizational profiles up-to-date. Good records lay the foundation for a successful development effort and are integral to the process of research.

When you are estimating how many researchers you will need, consider these factors also. A decentralized organization will probably require more research personnel than a centralized one. For example, during the last campaign at the University of Pennsylvania, our development department was centralized. There were five people on the research staff. As the campaign drew to a close, one research position was eliminated. After the campaign, Penn moved toward decentralization. Today, the university has incorporated a decentralized development department within a centralized structure. The research staff has grown to accommodate the needs of the development officers in the 13 schools and responsibility centers, as well as the needs of the central office. Currently, there are seven researchers on the staff, and we will have to add support for the upcoming campaign in the School of Arts and Sciences.

I suspect that as you see the dollar signs mounting, you will begin to wonder if all that time and staff support are really necessary for a successful campaign. But I think you will understand more clearly what is involved if we examine what hap-

Individuals	Corporations	Foundations
Full name	Full name	Full name
Nickname(s)	Trade name(s)	
Location of home(s)	Headquarters and local address	Principal office
Telephone numbers	Telephone number(s)	Telephone number
Place and date of birth	Founder	Donor
	History	History
Family background	Family relationships (if any)	Family relationships (if any)
Education		
Military service	Officers	Officers
Religious preference	Directors	Directors/trustees
Political affiliations		
Occupation/profession	Lines of business	Areas of interest
Business title		
Income	Net sales	Gifts received/ income earned
Assets or net worth	Net income	
Giving potential	Earnings outlook	Assets
Giving inclination	Contributions budget	Grant disbursements
		Grant appropriations
Business/professional associations	Local interests	Local interests
	Policies/procedures	Policies/procedures
Directorships/ trusteeships		Dates of board meetings
Club/organizational memberships	Grant patterns	Grant patterns
Honors received	Corporate image, actual and desired	
Avocations		
Relationship with your institution	Relationship with your institution	Relationship with your institution

Figure 5: Level 2 Research Elements

43

pens in Level 2 research. Figures 6 and 7 at the end of the chapter outline the sources you can use to find the necessary elements for Level 2 research for individuals and corporate and foundation prospects.

You will see that I've listed many more sources of information about individual prospects. This is mainly because these sources provide a less complete profile than corporate and foundation sources provide for their subject. And corporate sources are less complete than those for foundations. As you can see from the sources listed in Figure 7, four or five publications provide most of the necessary information on foundations.

After reviewing this list of sources, you will understand how the University of Pennsylvania can spend $80,000 per year on resource materials. But don't despair if your institution is unable to afford this. At the end of this chapter is a list of basic resources for an acceptable development library at a minimum of investment. I've starred the most relevant and cost effective. You can buy these resources for $1,000 to $2,000, and you can find many of the others at college or local libraries.

In today's world, you must also consider automated information systems. There are several very useful on-line data bases available. Most of these services have no start-up fee and charge only for the telephone call and usage time. You can identify potential foundation funding sources through the on-line *Foundation Directory* in about 15 minutes at a cost of approximately $15. Performing this same research manually could take up to a week at a much greater cost of labor. Following the list of basic resources is a list of eight data bases germane to fund raising.

The success of your capital campaign will depend on the quality of your research—on knowing whom to ask and for how much. If your research function is weak or nonexistent, it's time to reassign or hire staff for this vital task. If yours is a vital ongoing research operation, you're already one step ahead of the game. You can base your campaign strategy on the thorough knowledge of your prospects that results from good research.

Editor's Note: For more about this crucial aspect of capital campaigning, order CASE's Prospect Research: A How-to Guide. *This book provides the basics you need to build a fact-finding research program. To order send $20.50 (prepaid, includes shipping) to* CASE *Publications Order Department, 80 S. Early St., Alexandria, VA 22304.*

Figure 6: Sources of Information on Individual Prospects

Full name and Nickname(s)
Internal sources

Location(s) of home(s)
Internal sources
Social Register
Who's Who in America, etc.

Telephone numbers
Internal sources
Local telephone directory
Social Register

Place and date of birth
Internal sources
Who's Who in America, etc.

Family background
Who's Who in America, etc.
Social Register
National Cyclopedia of American Biography

Education
Internal sources
Who's Who in America, etc.
Who's Who in America, College Alumni Directory
Social Register
Alumni directories
Dun & Bradstreet Reference Book of Corporate Managements
Martindale-Hubbell Law Directory
Directory of Medical Specialists
Standard & Poor's Register of Corporations, Directors and Executives

Military service
Internal sources
Who's Who in America, etc.
Dun & Bradstreet Reference Book of Corporate Managements

Religious preference
Internal sources
Who's Who in America, etc.

Political affiliations
Internal sources
Who's Who in America, etc.

Occupation/profession
Who's Who in America, etc.
Dun & Bradstreet Reference Book of Corporate Managements
Martindale-Hubbell Law Directory
Directory of Medical Specialists
Standard & Poor's Register of Corporations, Directors and Executives
American Banker Directory of U.S. Banking Executives
Directory of Directors in the City of New York and Tri-State Area
The National Directory of Certified Public Accountants
Pro File
Who's Who in Real Estate
AMVA Direcory
Security Dealers of North America

Business title
Who's Who in America, etc.
Dun & Bradstreet Reference Book of Corporate Managements
Martindale-Hubbell Law Directory
Directory of Medical Specialists
Standard & Poor's Register of Corporations, Directors and Executives
American Banker Directory of U.S. Banking Executives
Directory of Directors in the City of New York and Tri-State Area
The National Directory of Certified Public Accountants
Pro File
Who's Who in Real Estate
AMVA Directory
Security Dealers of North America

Income
Corporate proxy statements
Internal sources (alumni questionnaires)
Periodicals

Assets or net worth
SEC Reports
Forbes 400

Giving potential
Internal sources including screening

Giving inclination
Internal sources

Business/professional associations
Who's Who in America, etc.
Standard & Poor's Register of Corporations, Directors and Executives
Proxy statement
Directory of Directors in the City of New York and Tri-State Area
Martindale-Hubbell Law Directory
Directory of Medical Specialists

Directorships/trusteeships
The Foundation Directory
Taft Foundation Directory
Foundation Center Source Book Profiles
Who's Who in America, etc.
Standard & Poor's Register of Corporations, Directors and Executives
Directory of Directors in the City of New York and Tri-State Area
Dun & Bradstreet Reference Book of Corporate Managements

Club/organizations memberships
Who's Who in America, etc.
Social Register

Honors received
Internal Sources
Who's Who in America, etc.

Avocations
Internal sources (including visitations and questionnaires)

Relationship with your institution
Internal sources

*Figure 7: Sources of Information
on Corporate and Foundation Prospects*

Corporations	Foundations
Full name	**Full name**
Standard & Poor's Register of Corporations, Directors and Executives	*The Foundation Directory*
Moody's manuals	*Taft Foundation Directory*
Dun & Bradstreet Million Dollar Directory	Local foundation directories
Local corporate directories	*Foundation Center Source Book Profiles*
State industrial directories	*National Data Book*
Trade name(s)	
Moody's manuals	
Annual reports	
Directory of Corporate Affiliations	
Headquarters, local addresses, and telephone numbers	**Principal office, telephone number**
Directory of Corporate Affiliations	*The Foundation Directory*
America's Corporate Families: The Billion Dollar Directory	*Taft Foundation Directory*
	Local foundation directories
	Foundation Center Source Book Profiles
	National Data Book
Founder	**Donor**
Moody's manuals	*The Foundation Directory*
Business Information Report (Dun & Bradstreet)	*Taft Foundation Directory*
	Local foundation directories
	Foundation Center Source Book Profiles
History	**History**
Moody's manuals	*The Foundation Directory*
Business Information Report (Dun & Bradstreet)	*Taft Foundation Directory*
Annual reports	Local foundation directories
	Foundation Center Source Book Profiles
Family relationships (if any)	**Family relationships (if any)**
Proxy statement	*The Foundation Directory*
Standard & Poor's Register of Corporations, Directors and Executives	*Taft Foundation Directory*
Dun & Bradstreet Million Dollar Directory	Local foundation directories
Business Information Report (Dun & Bradstreet)	*Foundation Center Source Book Profiles*
Moody's manuals	

Officers/directors
Annual report
Proxy statement
Moody's manuals
*Dun & Bradstreet Million Dollar
     Directory*
*Standard & Poor's Register of Corpo-
     rations, Directors and Executives*
*Dun & Bradstreet Reference Book of
     Corporate Managements*
Business Information Report
     (Dun & Bradstreet)
Disclosure

Lines of business
Annual report
Moody's manuals
*Standard & Poor's Register of Corpo-
     rations, Directors and Executives*
Business Information Report
     (Dun & Bradstreet)

Net sales/net income
Annual report
Moody's manuals
Dun's Business Rankings

Earnings outlook
Annual report
Moody's manuals
*Moody's Handbook of
     Common Stocks*

Contributions budget
Taft Corporate Directory
*Corporate 500: The Directory of
     Corporate Philanthropy*
*The CFAE Casebook: A Cross-Section of
     Corporate Aid to Education
     Programs*

Local interests
Taft Corporate Directory
*Corporate 500: The Directory of
     Corporate Philanthropy*

Officers/directors/trustees
Annual report
The Foundation Directory
Taft Foundation Directory
Local foundation directories
*Foundation Center Source Book
     Profiles*
IRS Form 990

Areas of interest
The Foundation Directory
Taft Foundation Directory
Local foundation directories
*Foundation Center Source Book
     Profiles*

Gifts received/income earned
Annual report
The Foundation Directory
Taft Foundation Directory
*Foundation Center Source Book
     Profiles*
IRS Form 990

Assets
Annual report
The Foundation Directory
Taft Foundation Directory
Local foundation directories
*Foundation Center Source Book
     Profiles*
IRS Form 990

Grant Disbursements
Annual report
The Foundation Directory
Taft Foundation Directory
Local foundations directories
*Foundation Center Source Book
     Profiles*
IRS Form 990

Local interests
Taft Foundation Directory
*Foundation Center Source Book
     Profiles*

Policies/procedures
Taft Corporate Giving Directory
*Corporate 500: The Directory of
    Corporate Philanthropy*
*National Directory of Corporate
    Charity*

Grant Patterns
Taft Corporate Directory
*Corporate 500: The Directory of
    Corporate Philanthropy*

**Corporate image, actual
and desired**
Annual report

**Relationship with your
institution**
Internal sources

Policies/procedures
Taft Foundation Directory
*Foundation Center Source Book
    Profiles*
Local foundation directories
The Foundation Directory

Grant Patterns
Taft Foundation Directory
*Foundation Center Source Book
    Profiles*
The Foundation Grants Index

**Relationship with your
institution**
Internal sources

Suggested Basic Resource Materials

* *Who's Who in America* and related directories (Marquis Who's Who, Inc.)
    Two-volume biennial compendium of some 75,000 biographies. Related
    works include regional directories, occupational/professional directories, and
    Who's Who of American Women.

* *Social Register* (Social Register Association)
    Long the arbiter of "society." Published in one volume since 1977 and still
    confined to 13 cities: Baltimore, Boston, Buffalo, Chicago, Cincinnati,
    Cleveland, Dayton, New York, Philadelphia, Pittsburgh, St. Louis, San Fran-
    cisco, and Washington, DC.

Directory of Medical Specialists (Marquis Who's Who, Inc.)
    Biographical sketches of over 290,000 physicians certified by any of the 23
    specialty boards of the American Board of Medical Specialties.

Martindale-Hubbell Law Directory (Martindale-Hubbell, Inc.)
    Educational, professional, and credit-worthiness data on attorneys arranged
    by firm within city and state. Midyear supplements available.

* Telephone directories
    The oft-forgotten white pages should not be overlooked as a research tool.
    Often, especially in large city directories, occupational clues will be found
    for accountants, attorneys, and real estate or securities brokers, among others.
    Bell & Howell Company markets a "Phonefiche" service that enables a sub-
    scriber to acquire a comprehensive collection of U.S., Canadian, and Euro-
    pean directories at a cost comparable to that charged by telephone companies
    for hard-copy directories; this saves space and ensures automatic receipt of
    new directory editions as they are published.

Standard & Poor's Register of Corporations, Directors and Executives (Standard & Poor's)

> Annual (January). Volume 1 contains basic data on about 45,000 major companies. Geographic, SIC, subsidiary cross-reference, obituary, and new listings indices in Volume 3, and biographical data on 70,000 executives and directors in Volume 2. Quarterly supplements.

*State industrial directories (MacRae's Blue Book Inc., etc.)

> Adjuncts to larger reference works, offering coverage of smaller firms, subsidiaries, divisions, etc. Available for most states, usually arranged by county and indexed alphabetically and by industry. Microfiche subscription service available from Colt Microfiche Corporation.

The CFAE Casebook: A Cross-Section of Corporate Aid-to-Education Programs (Council for Financial Aid to Education)

> Biennial. Descriptions of educational support programs of about 250 selected major corporations and corporate foundations. Indexed by type of business, by size of educational support program, and by field of giving.

Corporate 500: The Directory of Corporate Philanthropy (Public Management Institute)

> Descriptions of giving programs of 711 U.S. corporations, with a special focus on support for arts organizations and arts activities (policies, procedures, recipients, evaluative criteria).

National Directory of Corporate Public Affairs (Columbia Books, Inc.)

> Annual. Catalog of 1,500 companies with public affairs programs, including data about Washington offices, political action committees, corporate foundations, publicly circulated periodicals, and public affairs personnel. Alphabetical index of 10,000 corporate public affairs professionals.

Taft Corporate Information System (Taft Corporation)

> Profiles over 400 corporate contributions programs, with background data on corporate foundations and their sponsoring companies. Indexed by state, types of recipients, types of grants, sponsoring companies, corporate operating locations, individuals (name, place of birth, alma mater). Includes *Corporate Giving Directory* and two monthly periodicals, *Corporate Giving Watch* and *Corporate Updates*.

On-line Data Bases Germane to Fund Raising

Bibliographic Retrieval Services
> *Dow Jones News*
> *American Men and Women of Science* (R. R. Bowker)

Dialog Information Retrieval Service (Lockheed Missiles & Space Company, Inc.)
  Disclosure
  Encyclopedia of Associations (Gale Research)
  Foundation Directory (Foundation Center)
  Foundation Grants Index (Foundation Center)
  Grants Database (Oryx)
  National Foundations (Foundation Center)
  National Newspaper Index (Information Access)
  Newsearch (Information Access)
  Spectrum Ownership Profiles (Computer Directions Advisors)
  Who's Who in America (Marquis Who's Who)

Dow Jones News Retrieval Service (Dow Jones & Company, Inc.—Information Services Division)
  Barron's
  Disclosure
  Dow Jones Newswire
  Media General
  Wall Street Journal

Dun's Quest/Dunsprint (Dun & Bradstreet Credit Services)
  Dun & Bradstreet

NEXIS (Mead Data Central, Division of Mead Corporation)
  New York Times Information Bank

SDC Search Service (System Development Corporation)
  Grants Database (Oryx)

The Source (Source Telecomputing Corporation, a subsidiary of Reader's Digest Association, Inc.)
  Various news and business services

VU/Test Information Services, Inc. (Knight-Ridder Newspapers, Inc.)
  Philadelphia Daily News
  Philadelphia Inquirer
  Wall Street Transcript
  Washington Post

Chapter 8

Prospect Screening and Evaluation

Ann W. Caldwell
Vice President for Resources
Wheaton College, Massachusetts

T oday, in the age of information, the systematic collection, analysis, and storage of information provides the foundation for many a course of action. So too should capital campaigns be built upon a solid information base—and the most effective way to establish that base is through the screening and evaluation of prospects.

In its simplest terms, the objective of prospect evaluation is to identify the top 20 percent of your donor prospects and thereby enable you to target your resources to maximize participation of this group of donors in your campaign. The identification and evaluation of top donors should be an ongoing aspect of any development program before, during, and between campaigns. But to provide the groundwork for a major capital campaign, you will need a more formal prospecting program that involves a large number of volunteers and staff in the systematic screening of your entire constituency or a significant portion of it. A prospecting program may supplement and complement the findings of a feasibility study or it may even take the place of a feasibility study. It should enable you to discover new and previously unrecognized sources of support as you prepare donors, volunteers, and staff for the work of the campaign.

Prospecting can and should be more than a technical exercise. A well-orchestrated prospecting program should achieve the following goals:

1. *Identify volunteer leadership*. Involving a large number of individuals in the prospecting enables you to assess those who may become your most effective volunteer leaders and solicitors. And when you are rating your constituency for their giving capability, you can identify those with fund-raising experience and those who are likely to be the most influential with your top prospects.

2. *Provide staff with field training.* We often rely on staff who have had no campaign experience or who are new to our institution and constituency. Involvement in prospecting gives them valuable exposure to alumni and other constituents, helps them learn about and become acquainted with potential donors and volunteers, and gives them experience in representing your institution to others.

3. *Educate potential donors and volunteers about the campaign.* Every prospect screening session should include a brief overview of your institution's priorities and future needs. At Wheaton, when we realized that for the first time our campaign would place major emphasis on increasing the endowment, we developed a brief slide show to give at the beginning of each prospecting meeting. The slide show presented the history of the endowment and its role in the financial affairs of the college but made no direct appeal for gifts.

Prospecting gives you an opportunity to educate future donors and volunteers about the many ways of giving to your campaign, including planned giving. A prospect's rating may be quite different when you have explained to him or her that the institution is interested in multi-year pledges, life-income gifts, or even bequest intentions.

4. *Test the organizational framework for your campaign.* If you are planning to organize donor solicitation geographically, you may discover through prospecting that your constituents know far more about their classmates than they do about other alumni in the same city. In this case, reunions may be a better structure for your solicitation effort. You may learn that neighboring communities have so little in common that an area campaign would be folly.

5. *Update your records.* No matter how recently you have undertaken an alumni questionnaire or how good your system of tracking alumni, you probably still have gaps in your records. A good prospecting meeting will be certain to provide new information about the whereabouts, marital and family status, and business or professional accomplishments of your alumni.

6. *Raise sights.* Involve everyone in the prospecting program who is essential to the success of your campaign—staff, trustees, potential donors, and volunteers. And share widely with them the results of their collective effort. In this way, you will give them a sense of investment and confidence in the campaign. In some cases, participants in the prospecting program may have had no idea of the number or prominence of your alumni and other constituents. By creating that awareness you motivate them to work for the success of the campaign.

Wheaton College had not had a capital campaign since the mid-sixties. During those 20 years, the alumnae body had doubled. The growth of alumnae activities and clubs had not kept pace with this rapid growth, and therefore many alumnae around the country were unaware of one another. In fact, some knew each other socially or professionally but had no idea they were both Wheaton alumnae. When we showed alumnae a computer printout of 200 or more alumnae and parents in their immediate area, they were surprised at the extent of Wheaton's potential influence. And when they began to identify prominent individuals ("I didn't know *she* went to Wheaton!"), their sights were permanently raised.

Organizing a prospecting program

The first step in organizing a prospecting program is to define the prospect universe. The prospect universe should encompass all of the individuals to whom you will look for donor support during the campaign. It may include alumni, past and present parents, friends, faculty (including emeriti), and staff. The number of people in your prospect universe will determine the scope of your prospecting program.

Our prospect universe at Wheaton was 16,000 individuals. We divided this group into nine regions, based on geographic location. Because our alumnae are heavily concentrated in New England and the Northeast, some states, such as Massachusetts and Rhode Island, constituted a region all by themselves. Other regions, such as the Far West, were comprised of several states where alumae were more widely scattered. We then divided each region into areas with an average of 200 prospects each. We had 70 areas altogether. Sorting by ZIP code, we defined areas in terms of towns or neighborhoods (for large cities). We planned a prospecting committee meeting in each area.

You might want to organize your prospecting program by class structure, rather than by geographic location. You would identify leadership for decades of alumni classes, for example, and for each class. This may be an effective approach if your most successful capital fund raising has been done through the classes and in conjunction with reunions, and if you plan to organize your campaign solicitations on a class-by-class basis.

Class-based prospecting can have its pitfalls, however. First, those involved in class fund raising may be so familiar with the giving history of their classmates (largely through the annual fund) that they are unable to see potential. Secondly, class leaders may be scattered geographically and may not know about uninvolved classmates with high potential in other parts of the country. And because of their scattered locations, it may be hard to assemble class leaders for a prospecting meeting or, later, a campaign event.

However you organize your prospecting effort, you will need to identify volunteer leadership, beginning with the appointment of a national prospecting chair. The national chair recruits regional and area chairs. Prospecting leaders should be drawn from the ranks of those who are prominent in their local communities or professions and who have demonstrated a commitment to the institution either through past volunteer service or giving or both.

Each prospecting leader must recruit a committee. He or she works closely with a staff person who provides a list of suggested committee members, all drawn from the prospect list. Committee members should reflect the diversity of the prospect list in terms of age, geographic distribution, and type of affiliation with the institution (alumni, parents, or friends). Attorneys, financial and corporate executives, and volunteer community leaders should be involved because they are often in a position to know or judge the financial status and philanthropic interests of others. It's important to involve the most influential members of your constituency who are the peers of other potential major donors.

Each prospecting committee should include one committee member for every 20 or so prospects to be evaluated. A committee of 10 can handle approximately

200 prospects although many a successful prospecting session has been held with a smaller number of volunteers.

The prospecting meeting

The prospecting meeting should last about three hours. The volunteer leader, either alone or with the staff person, begins with a general introduction, describing plans for the campaign. He or she explains how the prospecting information will be used to finalize the campaign goal, shape its organization, and develop solicitation strategies for the top prospects. The agenda should allow time for questions from the committee members. The leader may also need to reassure those who are unfamiliar or uncomfortable with the idea of rating other people.

The rating process itself should take no more than two and a half hours. Even in the best of circumstances it can become very tedious indeed. Each committee member should have the following information:

1. A list of all individuals to be reviewed with home address, business address and title, and year of graduation or, for parents, student's name and year of graduation. It is better not to provide any additional information, such as prior giving history or volunteer activities as this may influence the rating committee. For example, they might underrate an alumnus from a wealthy family who has had no involvement with your institution since graduation while overrating a loyal volunteer with a 20-year record of annual giving. Those ratings could cause you to misdirect later efforts in the cultivation and solicitation of donors.

2. A rating information sheet or card that describes the gift ranges and lists the questions for rating. It should include the following basic points, but the details should reflect your institution's situation and campaign:

• Does this person have the capability of making a gift of $1,000; $10,000; $50,000; $100,000; $250,000; $500,000; $1 million or more?

• Does this person have any special interests related to the campaign goals: scholarships; faculty salaries and research; library; student activities; athletics?

• Would you be willing to solicit this individual? If not, who is likely to be the most effective solicitor?

• Would this individual make a good campaign volunteer/leader?

• Would you be willing to supply additional information about this individual that might be pertinent to this campaign?

• Do you know alumni or others affiliated with the institution who have the giving capability indicated above?

After the volunteer has answered these questions, he or she must consider and answer the most important question of all: "If our institution were at the top of his or her charitable priorities, what would be the largest gift this individual could make to this campaign?"

The leader should instruct prospecting volunteers to consider only financial information and not speculate about the prospect's motives and attitudes. The rating is for *capability*, not inclination or willingness to support the institution. It may not be easy to persuade the raters to focus on financial ability and disregard motivation, but it is essential. Prospecting seeks to discover the maximum potential for support. When this has been done, it is the task of campaign solicitors to create or enhance the inclination to give.

Group screening vs. silent screening

Prospecting volunteers can accomplish the rating in two ways: group screening or silent screening.

In group screening, participants arrive at a consensus through discussion. In this situation the more experienced and confident volunteers take the lead and encourage others to share their information. Group screening makes everyone aware of the collective potential for donor and volunteer leadership and thus serves as a sight-raising tool. Finally, group screening gives the staff and prospecting leader a chance to evaluate the quality of each volunteer's rating when he or she expresses and justifies it.

Silent screening has the advantage of preserving confidentiality, and this may encourage some volunteers who are not as confident or who have knowledge they don't want to share aloud. Silent screening may help discourage rating based on speculation, e.g., "That looks like a good street address—let's rate him an X."

And silent screening is essential for self-rating. You will want to ask your volunteers to rate themselves after they have rated everyone else. This conveys the important message that *everyone* will be asked to support this campaign according to his or her capability. While the results of self-rating are likely to be uneven, they give you insight into how some of your better prospects view their role as donors to the campaign. You must encourage them, however, not to view a self-rating as a campaign pledge.

Prescreening

If your alumni and parent constituency is too large for you to evaluate through prospecting, your staff may do prescreening. This may consist merely of removing all nondonors—the "never-nevers"—from your lists. Or you may want to target only constituents in certain large cities where you know you have both strength in numbers and a strong volunteer corps.

Some institutions use sophisticated computer analysis to preselect prospects on the basis of demographic data about per capita income in certain regions of the country. Or you may want to preselect those individuals with regular or significant past giving histories. Finally, you may want to limit your prospect universe by age, and assume that alumni who have graduated within the last 10 years are unlikely to be major gift prospects.

While prescreening may limit your opportunity to discover unknown or unexpected sources of support, it may be the only practical way to create a manageable prospect universe.

Some do's and one don't

Do have a detailed organizational plan for your prospecting program with a calendar of deadlines. Otherwise, prospecting can drag on forever and you'll never turn the information into a campaign.

Do make certain that your information system is in order and that it can produce lists in the quantity and format you need for prospecting as well as for recording and analyzing the rating information. The prospecting program will test your system capability—but it is a test well worth taking *before* the campaign is in full swing.

Do communicate clearly and often with your prospecting volunteers, describing what their job is and how it fits into the planning for the campaign, informing them about major developments on campus, and thanking them for the work they do. Today's prospecting volunteers are your institution's campaign solicitors and donors of tomorrow.

Do assure prospecting volunteers that the information they supply will be treated confidentially and will not be publicly attributed to them, but make sure they understand it will be used by staff and volunteers to develop the most effective solicitation strategies.

Do try to put some fun into the prospecting program. One national prospecting chair was pictured in the alumni magazine wearing a miner's helmet with headlight and wielding a shovel. Another was given complete fishing gear at a trustees' meeting, and all of the trustees were given lures. If your key volunteers find prospecting a grim and unrewarding business, they are not likely to respond with enthusiasm when you attempt to recruit them for the campaign itself.

Don't expect your prospecting program to provide all you need to know about your top prospects. The information uncovered through prospecting is only as good as the research that follows to validate the ratings and develop in-depth profiles and solicitation strategies.

How to follow up on prospecting results

You need to confirm and augment the initial discovery and rating of a large number of prospects. You can do this through the steps listed below:

• *One-on-one evaluation*: Staff or volunteers review selected lists of individuals with those who know them best. This might involve returning to a prospecting volunteer for more in-depth information. Or you might ask a class officer or fund agent to review a class list. A long-time faculty member could evaluate a list of majors in his or her department, or the chair of the last campaign could rate former major donors and volunteer leaders. In each case, the one-on-one evaluation should provide more detailed information about top prospects' sources of wealth and their interests and activities.

• *Research:* Every rated prospect should be researched to verify and elaborate on the rating.

• *Major prospect review:* The top 2 percent of your rated prospects will become your major gift list. The staff, trustees, and campaign leaders should review this list thoroughly (and often) in one-on-one evaluations and in group settings to uncover high-level contacts and connections to individual prospects. It is this small group of prospects who alone will determine the success or failure of your capital campaign.

At the same time that individual prospects are being screened and evaluated, you should be developing a list of corporate and foundation prospects. This is largely an internal staff function; much of the information about giving practices and criteria used by corporations and foundations is available through readily accessible sources. Identify through research a prospect list of corporations and foundations that are likely to support your institution either because of their own giving priorities or because of connections to your institution. Those connections may include past support, proximity to your institution, and representation on the board. Corporations that employ a large number of your alumni may be more likely to give. The size of grants typically made by the corporations and foundations on your list will make it relatively easy to identify those that are major prospects. Volunteers can screen the completed foundation or corporate prospect list. At this point you need to find out if a member of your board or other high-level volunteer can open a door for you or support your request for funding.

How to use prospecting results

Like a feasibility study, a prospecting program will provide you with essential information for finalizing the goal of your campaign. Because the information reflects prospects' maximum giving capability, it should reveal a potential far greater than your campaign goal.

You should balance maximum giving capability with a realistic staff projection of the outcomes of solicitation. If, as a general rule, only one in 20 of your major gift solicitations is successful, you may apply that ratio to the prospecting results. Or if your major gift prospect list is relatively small, you may want to analyze each individual prospect on the basis of a high/low expectation. To do so, you will need to factor in not only maximum philanthropic capability—the high expectation—but also what research and direct contact may tell you about the prospect's inclination to support your campaign goals—the low expectation. Figure 8 on the next page illustrates how we analyzed the prospecting results for the Wheaton campaign.

Once the campaign goal has been set, you can use prospect ratings to develop a gift table or pyramid of your campaign (see Figures 1 and 2, Chapter 7, for sample gift tables). The gift table, while demonstrating that the majority of the gifts must come from a very small number of donors, also reveals what size of gifts you will need and how many and, on the basis of prospecting results, what you can expect from your constituents.

Gift range	Number of gifts needed	Total individual capital gifts	Rated prospects	High hopes*	Low hopes*
$1,000,000 plus	4	$ 4,000,000	26	$27,500,000	$ 3,335,000
$500,000-999,999	5	$ 2,500,000	14	$ 6,575,000	$ 612,000
$100,000-499,999	29	$ 4,250,000	58	$ 7,300,000	$ 1,856,000
$50,000-99,999	25	$ 1,250,000	259	$ 7,168,000	$ 2,680,000
Major gift totals	63	$12,000,000	357	$48,543,000	$ 8,483,000
$10,000-49,999	125	$ 1,250,000	296	$ 2,590,000	$ 592,000
$5,000-9,999	250	$ 1,250,000	1,060	$ 2,783,000	$ 1,060,000
$1,000-4,999	1,000	$ 1,000,000	2,193	$ 1,919,000	$ 439,000
Special gift totals	1,375	$ 3,500,000	3,549	$ 7,292,000	$ 2,091,000
Individual capital totals	1,438	$15,500,000	3,906	$55,835,000	$10,574,000

*Prospects rated at $100,000 or above were individually analyzed for high/low hope. For all other rated prospects, the high hope was based on 35 percent of the prospects giving at the midpoint of the gift range and the low hope was based on 20 percent giving at the minimum gift range.

Figure 8: Wheaton Sesquicentennial Campaign: Gift Table vs. Prospect Potential

What others say about prospecting

The size of your institution and its fund-raising history should determine what kind of prospecting program you will use. An informal survey of six institutions of varying size, location, and character—Boston College, Pepperdine, Skidmore, Stanford, Tufts, and the University of Michigan—reaffirmed the value of prospecting but revealed considerable variation.

Some of the institutions try to give the prospecting meeting the most business-like setting possible. If the volunteer leader does not suggest a location, the staff selects an office, club, or hotel meeting room. These institutions avoid making the meeting a social affair, do not invite spouses (unless they are also alumni), serve no alcoholic beverages until the work of the meeting is completed, and seldom use private homes. However, if this is the preference of your institution, bear in mind that a good location can attract and impress volunteers. Whether using a business setting or a private home, aim for the best address.

The role of staff also varies, but several institutions rely increasingly on the support or direct involvement of the research department in prospecting. Schools and colleges that have very small research operations are expanding them to meet the demands of a campaign. Universities that have large research departments use them to coordinate the entire prospecting effort. The research staff is responsible for the process from beginning to end—from selecting the volunteer leaders, the sites, and the prescreeened lists to doing the follow-up one-on-one evaluations and research that refine and confirm the rating information.

Universities with very large alumni populations focus their efforts in one of two ways: Either they establish prescreening criteria that will generate a prospect pool at the highest level, generally $100,000-plus, or they select metropolitan areas with over 500 prospects or a standard statistical area with over 800. If there is known wealth in a city or town that does not have a large enough population to warrant a full-fledged prospecting session, prospecting is done through a combination of one-on-one evaluations and informal, small group evaluations.

Boston College uses this prescreening technique: The staff reviews a list of the entire prospect universe and identifies the top 100 names. These 100 names are given to every prospecting volunteer to review. The remainder of the list is broken into five parts, each of which is reviewed by at least four or five prospecting volunteers. In this way, new prospects surface, and the college is guaranteed a broad-based review of the major prospects.

Some colleges do not rate prospects for a specific gift range, but rather identify the minimum level for a major gift and screen prospects in this way. For example, if your institution considers $100,000 to be a major gift, you would ask, "Can this person give $100,000?" This focuses attention on capability rather than inclination. Volunteers often find it difficult to be specific about a range of capability, and frequently their estimates are too low. Using a single dollar figure for major gift rating helps volunteers assess capability. You can then determine the final target gift through staff review, follow-up interviews, and research.

Many colleges and universities attempt to discourage self-rating. Volunteers often say, "I know you will ask, so this is my range." Experience suggests that self-rating is generally five to 10 times lower than the individual's actual giving capability. And many volunteers feel that they have made their campaign commitment once they have rated themselves.

Although annual fund ratings rarely serve as the basis for capital solicitations, be sure that the annual fund and campaign offices share ratings and findings. It is not unusual to find that major capital prospects have not been rated as annual fund prospects and vice versa. You can deal with this problem by an internal review of gift histories, including an examination of cumulative giving as well as level and frequency of individual gifts.

Class volunteers may not necessarily be the best prospecting volunteers, according to many institutions. You may need to go through layers of class politics to reach a good screener. However, in major cities class screenings can help divide a large geographical list.

Institutions without a long history of capital fund raising and with a relatively young alumni constituency have found their prospecting works best when done by parents, who have had experience with their own alma maters, or friends of the institution who constitute the oldest, primary pool of major donors.

However you organize the prospecting program, it should provide the blueprint for your campaign organization, clearly indicating where to allocate your resources for maximum results. Prospecting gives you an opportunity to test all the ingredients necessary to a successful campaign—major gift potential, volunteer leadership and organization, information systems, communications, staff deployment, deadlines, and goals.

Chapter 9

The Role of the Board of Trustees

Henry D. Sharpe, Jr.
Vice Chancellor, Brown University
Campaign Chairman, The Campaign for Brown, 1979-84

" "A good trustee has to possess at least two of the three W's: work, wealth, and wisdom." This was the clear-eyed judgment of Dr. Henry Wriston, colorful president of Brown during my college years in the 1940s. Today, perhaps more than ever, we need trustees who will contribute whatever they possess of the three W's in organizing and executing a successful capital campaign.

Trustee work

Whatever else we might say about the work required in a capital campaign, it is physically demanding. The trustee puts in long hours of travel to countless meetings. The work is also psychologically demanding. Throughout the campaign, we put a premium on that scarce attribute: the ability to initiate action.

Trustee wealth

The wealth needed from the trustees is not only financial wealth but also wealth in spirit. The loyal trustee is not only asked to dig deep into his or her financial resources, but also to consider the effect of his or her contribution. A contribution has power far beyond its intrinsic worth. Its timing and size (and sometimes its matching conditions) can be an important inspiration to others, but more importantly, when the gift is given in the proper spirit, a thoughtful or handsome contribution is a joy to both the giver and the entire receiving community.

Trustee wisdom

And finally in a capital campaign, the trustee is called upon to exert wisdom on at least two levels. The trustee must participate in appraising the institution's overall financial condition to determine the soundness of its fiscal policies; and he or she must help the group make a wise (yet hopeful) assessment of the prospects for success of the proposed campaign goal.

On a more personal level, the trustee must use wisdom to devise viable approaches to each individual prospect whom he or she contacts. *Every* situation deserves the same level of sensitivity one would use in soliciting a wealthy, strong-minded alumnus whose favorite son or daughter has just been rejected for admission by the institution.

Capital campaigns, then, are the proving ground that determines how many of Dr. Wriston's three W's each trustee is able or (far more often) willing to contribute.

Setting the stage: Choosing a president

Trustees take the most important step in determining the success or failure of a major capital campaign long before the campaign itself is even considered. And that step is the choice of the institution's chief executive officer.

What are the qualities trustees should look for in a president? Three that are relative to fund raising often surface in trustee discussions. The first is simple: the ability to raise funds.

While this ability ranks very high indeed, trustees should not assign too much importance to this quality alone and in the abstract. Ability to raise funds is a very complex quality, especially in the highly volatile university context.

Of far greater fund-raising usefulness to an institution is a president's ability to unify a campus and carry it with him or her in good spirit. Not merely the trustees but the entire university community—alumni, faculty, and students—must be convinced of the need to support each other and to work together for common institutional goals.

For trustees to undertake successful fund raising without alumni support is the classic fruitless exercise. To do so without the backing of faculty is almost as unthinkable. And to undertake the fund-raising challenge without the infectious, if at times fractious, enthusiasm of the institution's students is to overlook another very helpful resource.

Evoking the spiritual dimension

Trustees should also look for a chief executive who has the ability to present the institution's case with spiritual dimension. That is, he or she must be able to articulate the institution's importance in terms that go beyond material appurtenances—endowments, scholarships, classrooms, laboratories, libraries, gymnasiums—to the loftier social goals that they are meant to serve.

A president must be able to communicate to society at large a sense of the institution's spiritual worth. More than anyone else, the president of an institution speaks for its ethos and spirit.

These two abilities—the power to unify an institutional community and to present the case with spiritual dimension—are, in my opinion, *the* fund-raising qualities trustees should seek in a chief executive. If the trustees are lucky enough to serve an institution with a chief who has these qualities, they are blessed indeed, for they can be certain that all the more mundane development matters will simply fall into place.

These trustees, or their predecessors, have already used wisdom in fulfilling one of their most critical roles—selecting a president. And they have also satisfied the first requirement of a successful capital campaign: They have placed the right chief executive on the job.

Defining the goal

After the choice of chief executive, the next step is to establish a clear definition of the campaign goal. To a large extent it is the president's responsibility to seek out, evaluate, and quantify the resources he or she believes are necessary to move ahead. The result is a "laundry list" of items with price tags. But don't confuse this with a capital campaign goal. To be sure, a proper goal is based on such a list, but it represents much more than the sum of the individual items. The goal is a moral statement. It is the embodiment of a reasoned and emotionally felt commitment by a caring, leadership group to raise the sum they have carefully evaluated, understood, and now accepted.

The path, moreover, "from laundry list to launch" is never totally predictable. It frequently leads to astonishing and unexpected outcomes. And it is at this point, when needs are being transformed into a goal, that trustees first become truly involved in the capital fund drive.

Two personal experiences illustrate how unpredictably trustees' conceptions develop during this early formative period. The first occurred while we were preparing for the Campaign for Brown. Just before new President Howard R. Swearer handed the Brown Corporation the first draft of his laundry list of projects, it was common wisdom among the trustees that "a successful $50-million capital fund drive is about the most the Corporation has a right to expect." When the Campaign for Brown actually began, however, our goal was $158 million. The total actually raised, $182 million—well over the original goal—further demonstrates the peril of drawing early conclusions.

While I was a trustee for an independent school, a very well-respected fund-raising consultant prepared a study that concluded, "The school has no hope of raising even $250,000." This was the minimum sum required to ensure the school's survival, according to an early laundry list. But the trustees, following the strength of their convictions, ignored the consultant's advice and bravely set a goal of more than $700,000. Perhaps not surprisingly, the goal was never reached, but the final sum raised was $505,000—more than double the amount the consultant had assured us was unattainable. The sum was enough to save the institution, which still survives in excellent health today, thanks to its trustees who so boldly shaped the outlines of a capital campaign.

Such wide discrepancies between initial concept, goal, and final result underscore the importance of trustee guidance and leadership during that most gelatinous period in a capital campaign, between laundry list and launch.

Balancing trusteeship and personal commitment

During this period each trustee is beginning to understand what his or her own participation in the planned campaign may have to be. It is at this point that trustees usually hear this "law" of capital campaigns: Individual trustees, or some closely akin core group, must personally raise something like 30 percent of whatever goal the trustees decide upon.

This is shattering news to all but the hardiest trustee, but it does seem to be more or less true. With trustee support at or close to that level, the capital campaign is virtually guaranteed to succeed.

The core group

Once the trustee has learned what is expected, he or she may draw little consolation from the information that family foundations or close relatives can help discharge this personal obligation. The result is hot discussion among trustees as to precisely what core group will be actually responsible for raising the key 30 percent.

In preparing the Campaign for Brown, for example, after much reflection we decided that the 54 active trustees did not possess the resources to account for anything like 30 percent of the anticipated goal. Therefore, we enlarged the core group by adding to it Brown's 104 living former (or emeriti) trustees. We hoped their added resources might bring us closer to the fabled 30 percent, but even with their help, we had to settle on a core-group goal of 19 percent of the overall proposed goal. This amounted to $30 million. In this case, therefore, the goal for core-group support was set at about as lean a level as good counsel would allow.

While the composition of the core group varies depending on each institution's particular situation, it is essential that the trustees identify *some* group as the core group. The group should be small enough to be truly loyal and manageable, yet big and wealthy enough to have a chance at raising that 30 percent.

Getting used to a goal

Once the core group has been defined, the reaction is likely to be: "We can't *possibly* raise that kind of money." Sometimes it's just a question of getting used to the idea, circling it a few times just as a dog who is about to lie down on a bed of leaves will circle it several times before he can settle down. He hasn't really done anything to make the leaves more comfortable. He just needed to get used to the idea. The trustees need to get used to the idea of their share of the goal. Once they have done this, the goal should become acceptable or even attractive to them.

Getting down to cases

In the Campaign for Brown, the trustees did their circling in a series of meetings where they contemplated what would be required of the active and emeriti trustees combined were they as a group to take on raising that $30-million 19 percent of the proposed goal. The purpose here was to get individual trustees to relate their own personal level of commitment to the needs of the university.

The first meetings, which involved only the active trustees, focused on helping trustees clarify in their own minds whether or not they felt they possessed the resources to raise about two-thirds of the proposed core-group campaign goal. We reviewed the personal implications of the money-raising challenge from many different angles.

First, we divided the active-trustee share of the core-group pie into the average gift from each active trustee. Then we divided the pie again after deducting some large gifts we hoped for from certain top prospects.

The meetings on these subjects divided the 54 active trustees into eight or nine groups of roughly 10 to 15 persons each. We deliberately made the groups overlap in membership so that each trustee was in several groups and probably attended two or three of these meetings. But each meeting brought together a different group of active trustees.

The subject of each meeting was the giving ability of trustees *not present*. All available published financial data about each of us was reviewed, and eventually the best possible matrix of information was constructed of each individual active trustee's potential resources. Far more important than the information we were gathering about the other trustees was the opinion each trustee was beginning to form about what his or her contribution would have to be to make the preliminary goal a reality.

It now became possible for the first time to make high-probability predictions of the contributing range (high, median, and low) of each active trustee. And it also became possible to gauge what, in fairness, we should each expect of ourselves.

Finally, during these meetings we learned a good deal about how the trustees got along with each other and which trustees would be the best possible solicitors for other members of the board.

A preposterous question

One of the exercises we did at these meetings illustrates poignantly how fluid a trustee's conception of his or her own contribution can be at this stage. Using past giving records, we determined for each trustee the amount of the largest-ever-made one-year dollar transfer to the university. We added these up and asked ourselves, "How much money would be raised if all the active trustees as a group were to give that same amount of money every year *for five years in a row?*"

At the time the question seemed almost too preposterous to ask, but, as it turned out, this impossible sum proved to be about 20 percent less than the goal the active trustees eventually imposed upon themselves and then went on to exceed.

This group success was built up from individual successes. I remember one particularly wealthy individual who was inspired by these preliminary meetings. Without any solicitation whatsoever, he voluntarily raised his planned gift of $250,000 to one well over $1 million. His revised gift included not only his own personal generosity but extensive help from an entirely new source, a related family foundation.

His new-found enthusiasm, moreover, caused him to structure the form of his donation carefully, using some unusually creative giving ideas. For example, through use of gifted insurance premiums, he not only pledged funds but endowed his continuing annual fund contribution. Thus his generous gift served as a model of sophistication to the other potential campaign donors.

These meetings—and their gratifying results—illustrate how skeptically you should regard early judgments of what a proper goal should be, and how generously trustees can respond when they clearly see the relationship between their own participation and the demands of the situation.

The product of these meetings was a reliable "ask" and "hope" for each active trustee, and the assurance, among the trustees themselves, that what each one was being asked to consider bore a definite relationship to what the others were being asked to consider.

Those important first solicitations

The next step is the solicitation, before the goal is set, of those who will be the pacesetters among the board. Here responsibility inevitably falls on the chair of the board of trustees, the campaign chair, and, most heavily, on the president. These three must, ex officio, asssume responsibility for making these earliest and most crucial solicitations of any campaign.

The information gathered in the self-appraisal conferences should be used to prepare attractive proposals for these initial contacts. If all the necessary facts have been gathered, it should be easy to frame the case for initial contributions.

While the importance of these first solicitations cannot be overemphasized, it's difficult to suggest any guidelines about the approach because each must be personalized to fit the prospect.

Setting the formal goal

Once these crucial initial solicitations have been done successfully, it is time to rally the whole core group so that each trustee can perform his or her two most important acts as a fund raiser: setting the goal for the whole campaign and deciding on his or her level of commitment. At this momentous point in the precampaign process, it is important to give these two steps special, even ceremonial treatment. Some institutions hold a retreat far removed from routine settings, often at a place that is exciting and interesting and also has some historic, nostalgic, or emotional significance to the institution.

This is an exciting occasion with full personal participation of the central element in the core group and, for the first time, the addition of the other members of the entire core group. Everything should come together at this moment to assure the support that will come as close as possible to raising the core group's 30 percent of the goal. Spouses also should be invited to this event. When proposed commitments are large, usually both spouses will be involved in deciding what the final figure will be.

We held the kickoff for the Campaign for Brown at a weekend retreat in Newport, Rhode Island, 30 miles away from the Providence campus. This setting has great historical significance for Brown. We scheduled daytime meetings—where much of the factual material was covered—in the function rooms of a large Newport hotel. And it was the trustees and not the professionals who stated the message. Several trustees, who happened to be from large corporations, related in their own words the story of the campaign so far—the many aspects of university need and the detailed organization of the upcoming drive. Although some board members were concerned that these presentations would be less than polished (and indeed some *were* rather "homespun"), I felt that this would lend a certain authenticity. The very lack of professional "slick" gave the presentations a genuineness and warmth that I believe helped ensure the final result.

After the presentations, the time came for the big decision: We set the actual goal for the campaign.

We chose Newport for our kickoff because it was there, in 1764, that the colonial legislature voted to approve the Brown University Charter. This historic vote took place in the old statehouse. It was particularly appropriate, therefore, that the ceremony at which we adopted the goal took place by candlelight in the very same legislative chamber of the statehouse where the charter had first been granted 215 years before. The scene was redolent with tradition and was indeed an unforgettable experience, welding together active and past trustees in a bond of common resolve and enthusiasm.

Yet we knew that behind the glamour and the emotion of this event lay the solid foundation of individual trustee commitment, developed during long months of hard work at core-group meetings.

Organizing for trustee solicitation

The goal was set, the trustees had a clear understanding of their own personal commitment, the wealthy and leading members of the board had made substantial and exemplary pledges. Now it was up to the active trustees to organize themselves for solicitation of the remaining members of the board.

Once the "asks" and "hopes" were developed, and the web of personal interrelationships between active trustees was understood, the solicitation responsibilities were assigned to appropriate board members.

With such data in hand, there were few mismatches. Delicate matters such as degree of commitment and appropriate peer group selection fell into place. Active trustee solicitation was completed briskly and with very encouraging results. We were at last ready for our efforts to spread outward through the rest of the core group to the emeriti trustees, with help from a growing group of new solicitors.

Trustee help in the general phase of the campaign

Trustee assistance is also the key to success in the solicitation of important donors in all other phases of the campaign. The president and the staff, no matter how experienced or skilled, cannot do everything required in the capital campaign. In fact, the trustee is the one person best able to tell an institution's story; no one else is closer to its reasons for making an appeal. Not only is the trustee best qualified to do this but the mere fact of his or her doing it has great value, both within the institution and in the outside world.

The involvement of trustees in the campaign is fairly straightforward. Long before the goal is set, the staff reviews and evaluates every resource the institution possesses. This takes painstaking research as imaginative and extensive as time and funds will permit. However, the rewards will not be long in coming as the value of a close interface between the leading prospects and the trustees becomes highly apparent. Throughout the campaign, frequent meetings should be held to strengthen this interface. It will become, as we will see, a major campaign resource.

For it is one thing for staff researchers to identify a rich person or an organization with an interest in biophysics. It is quite another to establish some profitable connection between that individual or organization and the institution. Here again the trustee is the vital link. More frequently than you might expect, there will be a personal relationship between a prospect and a trustee. It is amazing how often these unexpected relationships are discovered as researchers methodically sort names and prospects. And many of these turn out to be of enormous importance. At this stage of the campaign, moreover, the staff should have developed a series of mileposts to establish the number and value of pledges necessary by certain dates throughout the campaign. The trustees then review these mileposts and any deviations at regular campaign progress meetings.

70

Trustee help in remote locations

It is important to review the hometowns of board members to see who may become the focal point of fund-raising efforts in strategic but faraway places.

The campaign needs area chairs. Sometimes a trustee is willing and able to volunteer to be an area chair, but often, for various reasons, he or she lacks the time or ability to head the active effort. In this case, the trustee should help recruit a local chair and once this person has accepted the position, the trustee should provide support and assistance. For example, the trustee should help arrange local affairs to welcome the president of the institution or other institutional officials. Organized follow-up by local solicitors can then ensure that these events pay off in terms of successful solicitations.

The light touch

It's important to maintain a light touch with trustees throughout a campaign. Drives are hard work and, most of the time, not very exciting. Most people do not like to ask other people for contributions. Thus, the campaign needs plenty of opportunities—preferably dramatic—to recognize the trustees' contributions, and not just the financial ones.

The Campaign for Brown included many such motivational occasions. Particularly effective was the special musical show at the end of the drive. Participants included trustees and other major contributors, administrators, members of the faculty, students, and prominent volunteer officials of the campaign. An evening of fun and entertainment expressed the university's appreciation as everyone shared in good fellowship.

Staff/trustee relationships

Trustees often forget that staff too can use a little encouragement when the going gets tough or, for that matter, at any other time. Trustees who understand this fact can go a long way toward lightening the staff's sometimes difficult burden. Trustees can also be extremely helpful to senior administration by spotting staff problems early and working *constructively* toward straightening them out. A serious staff problem requires patience and understanding. Who should understand this better than a veteran trustee?

Conclusion

Following the procedure described in this chapter, the core group at Brown sparked a highly successful fund-raising campaign that eventually went 17 percent over its $158-million goal to raise just over $182 million.

It's true that the trustees' core-group goal had been set very conservatively, 19 percent of the total goal, far below the 30 percent many feel is critical. But Brown trustees went on to illustrate how important trustees can be to a university's fund raising once they hit their stride. Instead of raising the 19 percent, the core group actually raised 27 percent of the campaign goal. That is, 54 active trustee members of the core group supplied an *average* contribution of $655,555 for a total of $35.4 million. If we deduct two extremely large contributions from the total, the average is still high—$246,296 from each active trustee.

The 104 emeriti trustees of the core group (all of whom had served as active trustees at one time or another) gave an average of $70,192 each.

So the initial surmise that $50 million was probably all that could be raised from Brown's entire constituency proved conservative indeed. The core group of active and emeriti trustees did almost that well ($42.7 million) out of their own pockets and came very close after all (27 percent) to supplying the fabled core-group desideratum of 30 percent of the goal.

Far more important than their financial generosity, however, was the standard of commitment they set. Their enthusiasm and loyalty powered the largest and most vital capital campaign ever mounted by Brown University and made them a stunning illustration of how important the role of the board of trustees is in a capital campaign.

Chapter 10

The President's Role in a Capital Campaign

Edward T. Foote II
President
University of Miami

Immodest though it sounds, the transcending importance of the president to a capital campaign cannot be overemphasized. The campaign is the translation of a vision to the most demanding reality of all, money. The president is both the principal author of the vision and, as the university's chief advocate, the ultimate asker for big money.

The role of the president begins with a vision. Without vision, that image of an institution sometime in the future made better by people's generosity, the campaign is unlikely to succeed. People give money to support progress, improvements, increasing quality. They want to support winners. People give money for many reasons, but they do not give unless they believe in the cause.

The president is the architect of the cause. Many others help build the building, but he or she designs it. Each great American university had its visionary, inspirational leaders. During their tenure, the money flowed. The connection was not an accident, and it never is.

The president's vision is not only the blueprint but often the catalyst for institutional change. Universities are complex, cumbersome creatures. Among the characteristics of professors and students alike are deep skepticism about institutional change and limitless opinions. Ironically, many of the same brilliant people exploring the edges of changing knowledge in their own fields have little patience with changes in the institution that nurtures their work. And students who will spend four short years of undergraduate study are understandably more interested in what those years will mean to the quality of their own education than what an endowed chair may mean to their successors in the classroom a decade hence.

The president has no monopoly on ideas, but during his or her tenure, he or she alone occupies the office, the one intersection through which cross all roads within the university, and between it and the rest of the world. That is why the vision must begin with the president's lonely thinking.

If the thinking is clear and strong, even the commonplace will fit freshly into a new mosaic of an existing institution. Linked with imaginative new ideas, the ordinary shines with new attraction. This linkage between the existing and the possible begins the capital campaign.

The president must then translate the vision to the many constituencies of the university, modify the early ideas as may be appropriate, then prepare the institution for the campaign journey. The president must begin with the faculty, for the faculty, as the heart of the university, must be also at the heart of the vision. The president is responsible for synthesizing the dreams of deans and faculties into a coherent whole. Slick brochures and fancy videotapes, slogans and banquets cannot mask a vision without academic substance. The vision must be real, supportable, tangibly connected to the actual work of the university. Most donors, especially those capable of the largest gifts, are wise. If the story does not tell, the money will not come.

The process of creating, refining, and selling the vision is the second most fascinating part of the campaign (the first is raising and counting the money). For the University of Miami during its present capital campaign, this preliminary process took a full two years of thinking, debating, drafting, ordering priorities, sorting through countless needs—from buildings to scholarships—among the 14 colleges and schools of the university.

The next audience to convince, in many ways the most important, is the board of trustees. Especially at a private university, the board of trustees will make or break a capital campaign. Typically, trustees include people of accomplishment, wealth, and power. They must give generously themselves, and they must participate actively throughout the entire life of the campaign. Thus, well before the final burnishing of that guiding vision, the president must bring the trustees into the process, excite them about their own institution, and teach them about its strengths and weaknesses. The president must inspire them to discharge their fiduciary responsibility not timidly in the narrow financial sense, but boldly in the full sense of not only holding, but of building assets for the benefit of others.

The first phase of the president's responsibilities ends with the debate at the board level that brings together two bodies of work. The first reflects the actual needs of the institution, refined, supportable, and linking the reality of today with the possibilities of tomorrow. The second is how much money the university can possibly stretch to raise. The magnitude of the stretch is an essential part of the president's task at this stage. A campaign that reaches too low a goal is not a successful campaign. The president must advocate the risk of failure, or the goal will be too low.

The organization of the campaign, of great importance itself, is ultimately the president's responsibility. Dedicated trustees and loyal alumni are essential but not sufficient. A community proud of its university will make the president feel good, but unless the staff functions professionally, efficiently, and effectively, the campaign will not succeed.

After the president, the two most important officers in the campaign are the provost and the chief development officer. The provost should be mentioned first, because upon the provost as the president's chief operating officer will fall the many burdens shed by the president during the campaign. The provost must pick up the slack and alter his or her own responsibilities so that the president can lead the campaign. Thus, the relationship between the president and the provost must be strong and characterized by complete trust. Important business is, of necessity, done on the run. Often the unsung heroes of successful campaigns are not those making the speeches or sharing photographs with wealthy donors, but the provosts of American universities.

The chief development officer has the day-to-day responsibility for organizing and implementing the campaign. Selection of this officer is one of the president's most important jobs. The president works closely—frequently daily—with this officer. Together with the chief financial officer and the chief development officer, the president must first think through and then approve a realistic campaign budget. Here, the president's responsibilities are not to be penny-wise and pound-foolish. Major campaigns are expensive. The campaign budget must supplement normal development expenditures. It can be capitalized for accounting purposes, but it must cover the extra expenses of the campaign.

Depending upon its quality and structure, the development staff may have to be reorganized, its energies redirected. The big money is raised by presidents, trustees, and other powerful friends of the university. Peers are best to ask peers for large gifts. Each request is a separate, complicated chapter of the campaign. The organization of cultivation events is complex and time-consuming. Careful attention to detail pays.

The vision created and explained, the board of trustees convinced, the campaign goal set, and the staff organized, the president then turns a major part of his or her energies to getting the job done. Normally this begins with the board itself. Most people, even trustees, would not choose fund raising as their favorite pastime. Most would prefer to talk about other valuable human endeavors. Basic research, the quality of teaching, or the football team is always a more interesting subject than the gritty realities of asking people for money. Yet if all is well with the campaign, the trustees, despite this natural reticence, will enjoy a participant's excitement in a grand adventure.

Together with the chair of the board and/or the chair of the campaign, the president must be deeply involved in all key solicitations of trustees. People give to winners. People give to other givers, and if the trustees do not give, and generously, the campaign begins in trouble. Answerable to the trustees for the well-being of the institution, the president rightfully should turn to those same trustees and ask them to be answerable for a substantial portion of the campaign. Thus, for a long time, and with much planning and strategy, the president must work with key trustees to build the first and most important base.

Early on, the president learns that his or her own time is among the most important ingredients of a successful campaign. The reason for this is simple but bears emphasis. There is only one president. There is only one office where all of those institutional roads cross. The president symbolizes the university to the alumni, the corporate community, the world at large. The president must go to the community, the business leaders, the national community of foundations and multinational companies, and state the university's case.

Normally, the president will find a willing, if occasionally guarded, audience. Society treasures its colleges and universities. Neighbors will not like students parking on their lawns, fans will bemoan a losing football season, and occasional controversies will trigger strong reactions from the community, but basically people are proud of higher education. Pride is a strong asset in a campaign, and nurturing it is an important part of the president's responsibility. Pride depends in part on good news. Thus, news of the campaign as it unfolds must be communicated with an eye to its maximum impact. The place and timing of campaign announcements are important.

Every campaign, even the best, will have disappointments. The president is important also in helping the university through the difficult days. Most big campaigns last for five years or so. Inevitably, there will be slow periods when there is nothing much to report. It is then that the president has an additional responsibility: to keep the momentum going. The president may be disappointed, but must not show it. The president must encourage the dean who has just been turned down to try another donor on another day. The trustees' attention may drift away, and the president must invite it back. The professor whose new library wing is still only a dream must be encouraged to keep the faith. Students wondering why tuition is rising, despite all the money being raised, must be patiently educated about the complex realities of university financing.

The campaign takes on a life of its own. For the president, it becomes a job within the larger job, separate but closely related. Being chief executive officer of a major university fills the day well even without a capital campaign. Keeping an appropriate relationship between the campaign and the rest of the job, then, becomes one of the president's most difficult challenges. If the campaign becomes too all-consuming, the faculty, staff, and students lose their leader, and the university ultimately will be the loser. If, on the other hand, the president does not devote sufficient time to the campaign, the likelihood of its success will be slight.

During the height of the campaign, the president will spend as much as a third of his or her time on the campaign itself or directly related responsibilities. This requires first a clear understanding of both the university's priorities and the campaign's priorities. Nothing can fritter away a president's time as quickly as a major campaign. There is always something to do, another donor to see, another letter to write, another party to attend. Each day, one of the president's most important decisions will be simply the budgeting of time, deciding what to do or delegate.

The president will need strong staff support in this essential task of planning. From the chief development officer to the secretary, the president must be guided through the maze. As important as each volunteer thinks a project may be, not all projects are of equal importance. The president can attend only so many parties in one evening, one week, or one social season. The decisions must be made without offending. This is not easy, but the president must learn how. Typically, 10 percent of the donors will provide 90 percent of the capital funds raised in a major campaign. The president's time must be spent with the top echelon of these prospective leadership donors.

People do not give money to an institution they don't feel good about or close to, no matter how worthy it may be. They give money to institutions that reach out and make them feel welcome, important, and needed—because they are. Thus, a major part of the president's responsibilities is reaching out, identifying people who can make the campaign a success, then bringing them closer to the university. How this is done depends on the nature of the institution and the president. Here, also, staff work is essential. Small parties gathering not only potential donors but interesting academic, governmental, or artistic leaders are essential. Continuing communication with important prospects is a must. An understanding of their interests and desires is critically important.

The president's entertaining and other social responsibilities during the campaign require care lest consumption of calories be mistaken for effective fund raising. It is the quality, not the quantity, of the president's efforts that counts. Only a university president could know just how many parties there are on this planet. The president may be the biggest dud in town, but he or she will be invited to most of them by virtue of the office. Attending some will be important. Attending others will not.

Determining the importance among competing events is a complex and subtle process indeed. Who should go to what? If the president, the chair of the campaign, and key trustees are everywhere on the social scene, their significance is diminished. If the president especially is seen too little off the campus, that scarcity in the circles of those capable of giving money will be noticed. The president's challenge, therefore, is to be visible at the many functions—the right ones—enough but not too much. Often, a half-hour of visiting during cocktails before the banquet does just as much good as spending all five hours through the last speeches.

How and whom a president entertains at home are powerful chapters of each campaign. The "how" of this entertaining is a function of the personality, style, and taste not only of the president but of his or her spouse. The mood of a cocktail reception before a football game is very different from that of an intimate candlelight dinner for 12. The president's entertaining must include both kinds of functions and many others, but the most special parties must be reserved for the most special prospects and those whom they would enjoy.

The "whom" of presidential entertaining can make a difference in a big campaign. The staff work coordinated by the chief development officer is of the utmost importance. Before invitations are extended, the chemistry of the party must be fully understood. It is not enough just to invite potential donors. The party should be fun.

Sometimes it is appropriate to make a blunt pitch for funds, but at such small gatherings in the president's house, generally this is not effective. Rather, the ambience should include not only good fellowship but also at least some attention, directly or indirectly, drawn to the university. This can be done through the natural drift of conversations or, more specifically, through the use of student musicians or the like. When the guests leave, the point is that they not only had a good time, but feel closer to the university.

Each potential donor is different, and each must be treated differently, from cultivation to popping the question. The more the president, the chair of the campaign, and other key trustees know about a prospect, the more effective they will be. Thus, again, good staff work is critical. Confidential briefing memoranda should include every relevant detail, from financial worth to interests.

Who should ask for major gifts depends on which person, or people, will be most effective. Almost always, the president should be part of the team. And a team it may be, if an approach by several is judged to be the best way. People give to people, and they give in proportion to their respect not only for the institution, but also for the person who asks them. This respect will be the greater if the asker has put his or her money on the line in generous measure. The trustees must have made their own commitments to be effective.

The solicitation itself should be straightforward and businesslike. The place is important. A business lunch in pleasant surroundings is often a good setting, but some prefer a formal call at the donor's office. The solicitors, including the president, should be thoroughly prepared with the facts not only about the university and the need, but about the donor's needs and interests. Donors whose interest and needs mesh with those of the institution will generally make the maximum possible commitment. Most donors' needs include minimizing taxes, so some knowledge of alternative legal forms of gifts is important. Some donors think immediately of a gift of cash, but informal discussion about testamentary and planned giving, trusts, or appreciated property can yield much larger commitments.

Tempting as it is to rush the process, especially with a major donor, patience is usually better. There is a proper pace to all human communications. Fund raising is no exception. The same person who may give no more than $100,000 today may give $1 million two years from now if properly motivated in the cause. The stimulation of other large gifts, the momentum and excitement of the campaign all bear on each individual decision. The waiting period should include cultivation, from lunches to concerts or trips with the football team, and maximum, though often subtle, education about the university and its needs.

No president will do all of this with equal ability. Each president has strengths. Some like fund raising better than others do. But properly orchestrated, as only the president can do, a capital campaign is not only an important phase of the university's development, it is fun. Helping create a vision for a precious institution is deeply gratifying. Presidents will enjoy fund raising in direct proportion to their enjoyment of people because ultimately a capital campaign is as complex, as fascinating, occasionally as exasperating and disappointing, as people themselves. Whether or not to give money—and how much—is an emotional, personal decision, made for all of the infinitely varied reasons that people make decisions. Presidents who understand that will not only be more successful at fund raising, they will enjoy it more.

And when the money starts to flow, as it will for a campaign properly envisioned and led, the president's ultimate satisfaction is the result. For someone who has chosen the life of academic leadership, there is nothing quite so satisfying as announcing to the faculty that the new science building will actually be built. For people who believe in the importance of education and research, just imagining all those experiments to be conducted, the young minds to be strengthened over the coming generations is reward enough.

Chapter 11

Organizing Yourself for Major Gift Success

William F. Dailey
Principal Gifts Director
Stanford University

Twice during the past 25 years, Stanford University has completed capital campaigns of a magnitude never previously attempted by any university. The first was the $100-million PACE Campaign from 1961 to 1964; the second was the $300-million Campaign for Stanford from 1972 to 1977. As I write this chapter, Stanford's administration, development office staff, and volunteer leaders are in the final stages of a three-year planning process that will lead in 1987 to the public announcement of yet another capital effort of unprecedented scale, the Stanford Centennial Campaign. Thus, my participation in a book entitled *The Successful Capital Campaign* is nothing if not timely. The table of contents of this book has been the story of my life for the past three years.

As Stanford's principal gifts director, my personal involvement in our current precampaign planning has been focused on two areas: First, I am responsible for the preannouncement solicitation of nucleus fund commitments from those individuals with the capacity to make the largest gifts to our Centennial Campaign. At the same time, I have been assisting in the training of younger and newly hired staff in the theory and execution of successful large gift fund raising in a capital campaign setting. In other words, I try to practice what I preach.

This chapter contains highlights of the instruction I've been giving to the Stanford staff. Whether you are a newcomer to the field of large gift fund raising or a seasoned professional honing your skills, I hope my thoughts will help you to greater success and fulfillment in your work.

Fundamentals of major gift fund raising

This chapter deals only with soliciting gifts from individuals, not corporations or professionally managed foundations. A "personal foundation" is different. Don't be misled when an individual makes a gift through a personal foundation. These are still individual prospects and should be treated as such. Don't make a foundation-type approach to such a prospect.

Generally speaking, individuals make two types of living gifts (as opposed to gifts by bequest): the annual gift and the major gift. For the moment, let's forget about distinctions between types of large gifts—special gifts, major gifts, leadership gifts, and principal gifts. Whether the solicitation is for $50,000 or $50 million, the basic principles are the same.

Before you can understand large gift work you need to recognize the fundamental differences between annual and major gifts. These differences are listed on the next page. As you can see, about the only thing that annual gifts and major gifts have in common is their source—the individual donor. Practically every other element of the process is different.

The seven steps to a major gift

We can describe a successful major gift solicitation as the process of moving a prospect from interest to involvement to commitment. Here again, we see how major giving differs from annual giving: People make small annual gifts to projects in which they are "interested" or "involved." But they make large major gifts only to projects to which they are "committed."

A successful major gift solicitation may involve as many as seven steps, *but not every solicitation must begin with the first step.* Many situations are already well along in the process, and you should be able to recognize this fact.

The seven steps are as follows:
1. prospect identification;
2. research and qualification;
3. strategizing the approach;
4. involving the prospect;
5. making the ask;
6. closing the solicitation; and
7. after-solicitation follow-up.

None of these seven steps is original with me. Anyone who has sold any "bigticket item"—be it a major gift, an automobile, an expensive home, a large insurance policy, or a mainframe computer—will recognize these as the seven steps to any successful major sale.

Because a chapter could be written on each of these steps—and, indeed, other chapters in this book cover some of them—I will not examine each in depth. Rather, I will try to explain how you can use the seven steps not only to organize individual gift approaches but to organize your overall job as well.

Annual Gifts	Major Gifts
1. An annual gift is just that: a gift made regularly each year and ranging from $10 to $10,000.	1. A major gift is often—but not always—a one-time commitment of significant financial resources.
2. An annual gift is usually given in cash from current income.	2. A major gift is almost never made in cash—or, in other words, in after-tax dollars. Almost always, it is made from appreciated assets, usually either negotiable securities or real property, which would be subject to a capital gains tax if sold by the donor. Thus, major gifts are almost always made from capital, rather than from current income.
3. The donor motivation is a feeling of general loyalty to your institution. Consequently, most annual gifts are unrestricted to the university or unrestricted to a certain school or department.	3. While some major gifts are made on an unrestricted basis, more often a major gift is stimulated by the donor's interest in a specific subject area at your institution, such as art, medicine, science, and so on. Thus, most major gifts are restricted as to purpose.
4. Annual gifts are solicited once a year on a cyclical basis against a short-term deadline.	4. The financial circumstances of the donor usually set the timetable —at least in part—for a successful major gift solicitation. Thus, the length of a major gift solicitation can range (literally) from 30 minutes to a lifetime.
5. Depending on the volume of prospects and the type of program involved, annual giving volunteers usually complete from three to 25 solicitations each year.	5. Major gift volunteer assignments are usually made one at a time, on a priority basis. A volunteer seldom has more than three assignments at a given time.
6. Annual giving volunteers are usually expected to "close their own deals."	6. Because of the high stakes in-volved, a major gift volunteer needs a wide range of university resources ("closing help" from a university president, dean, trustee, or staff person, and so on).

Using the seven steps to organize yourself

During my 16 years of major gift work at Stanford University, I have observed many young and capable fund-raising professionals attempt to make the transition from annual fund to large gift work. Some have succeeded marvelously; others have not. Many of those who fail seem to share a common denominator. While annual fund work is largely process-oriented, the new activity, in their eyes at least, seems to have no such clear-cut "process to success." Because they've been told that every major gift solicitation is a separate mini-campaign of its own, they fail to recognize that there is a common process to guide them through each of these individual solicitations. That process consists of the seven steps. And not only do they apply to each individual solicitation, but they are the key to organizing a continuing work plan day by day, week by week, and month by month.

Let's assume that you find yourself assigned to a new geographic territory. Your major rated prospect list numbers perhaps 250, and you have basic research information about each prospect. Your assignment is to develop a steady stream of large gifts from these prospects, working against a stated deadline, such as the framework of a capital campaign. How do you begin?

First, determine how far on the list of steps each prospect has progressed. You can make this judgment on the basis of all the information available to you—prior giving records, the files in your office, conversations with your predecessor in the assigned territory and/or any good volunteers available to you, and whatever other sources you have.

Once you have each prospect located on the list of steps, you are ready to decide what comes next. And that will be whatever is necessary to move each person to the next step. For those who are merely identified (Step 1), you need to call for research (Step 2). For those who are identified and researched, you need to begin building your strategy (Step 3), and so forth. And—wonder of wonders—you will discover that some of your prospects are already identified, researched, strategized, and involved. In short, they are ready to be asked, and this should be done as soon as possible.

What I have described obviously requires a great deal of work and a good deal of time. And, of course, you can't do everything at once. But what you should do, now that you have organized your prospect body, is develop a daily, weekly, and monthly work plan that will enable you to use your time efficiently to move the best prospects through the seven steps quickly and effectively.

Don't waste your time worrying about where the next gift is coming from. If you spend your time deciding what the next step is for each prospect—and setting and meeting a deadline to accomplish it—the gifts will come automatically.

Some hard questions (and candid answers)

Question: When is the right time to make the ask?

Answer: As soon as you are ready—that is, as soon as you are at Step 5—and as long as there is no compelling reason *not* to ask. The ideal time to ask is when the prospect's financial fortunes have seen (or are about to see) a decided improvement, such as during a strong stock market or, even better, just before the sale of his or her company or stock therein for a large gain, where the capital gains tax can be at least partially offset by a big charitable deduction.

Don't use a generally weak stock market as a blanket excuse not to ask *anyone* for a gift. When some stocks go down, others go up. Which ones does your prospect hold?

A cardinal rule: When in doubt, go ahead and ask! Many more gifts have been lost because no one asked than have been lost by a poorly timed ask.

Question: How much should we ask for?

Answer: How much do you need? (No, I am not being facetious.) If you have assessed the prospect's capacity realistically and, in your judgment, he or she has the capacity to give what you need, ask for it. If it's impossible or unrealistic, you can always come down, but you can never go up.

Question: Please be more specific. If a given prospect has an identifiable net worth of $10 million, how much should we ask for in an outright (not deferred) gift?

Answer: My experience has been that it is a rare prospect who will consider an outright gift of more than about 5 percent of his or her net worth. Your prospect with a net worth of $10 million should be a reasonable prospect for an ask in the $500,000 range.

However, a prospect's total net worth is only one of several important factors you should consider. For example, a retired couple with no children and a net worth of $10 million might consider a gift of significantly more than $500,000. But consider a 45-year-old entrepreneur, who also has a net worth of $10 million but is married, has four children of precollege age, and has put all his assets into an ongoing business enterprise. He is more likely to be receptive to an ask of $25,000 to $50,000.

Question: You mentioned deferred gifts above. How do you feel about them in an overall large gift development program?

Answer: Deferred gifts can be extraordinarily useful by enabling a prospect who is financially comfortable but not truly rich to make a significantly larger gift on a deferred basis than he or she could make outright.

The greatest danger with deferred giving is that some staff members rely on it as a crutch to avoid making harder outright asks. I have seen a lot of potential gift money "left on the table" because a staff person opted for a deferred gift approach with a prospect who was perfectly capable of making a comparable outright gift. Use the deferred gift approach only when it is truly appropriate. Do not let deferred gifts "cannibalize" your much more useful outright gifts.

Question: Assume you have a prospect with a gift capacity of from $250,000 to $2 million. Who should make the ask? A volunteer? A university officer or trustee? A development staff person? Some combination of the above?

Answer: Each ask should be made by that person, or combination of people, with the best chance for an affirmative response. The problem with volunteers making an ask by themselves is that many of them either can't or won't do it. (For all of the reasons you have heard.) In my experience, the best asks have been made by a two-person team composed of a volunteer with strong influence on the prospect and the university person (officer, dean, faculty member) with the strongest interest in the proposal being advanced.

Avoid asks by more than two people. You don't want to seem to be "ganging up" on the prospect.

Question: If there is no good volunteer or available university officer or trustee to make the ask, should a development staff person do it alone?

Answer: Certainly, particularly if the alternative is that no ask is made. That's the cardinal sin.

Question: Should a large gift ask to an individual be made verbally or in writing?

Answer: Both, and in that order. First, the solicitor should ask for the gift face-to-face in a quiet and thoughtful setting. The verbal ask should then be followed by a letter from the asker, summarizing the earlier conversation, confirming the exact proposal, and requesting a positive response.

Corporations and foundations usually require formal written proposals. But when you are soliciting a living, breathing person, you should begin with a personal conversation and follow up with a timely written confirmation of the proposed transaction.

If you send a written large gift proposal to an individual without a prior personal conversation, you are just wasting time and paper.

Question: We've heard so much about "peer asking" over the years. Can someone who has never made a large gift ask another prospect to do so?

Answer: That depends on why the asker has never made a comparable gift. If he or she clearly has a gift capacity comparable to that of the prospect, but has never made a large gift, don't use him or her as a volunteer. (For reasons that should be obvious.) On the other hand, if the potential asker has given generously within his or her means, the volunteer has every right to ask someone else to make a gift that reflects that donor's capacity.

Obviously, the best volunteer asker is someone who is both a peer of the prospect and who has already made a gift of the same magnitude. But as we all know, these ideal volunteers can be few and far between.

Now that we've gone over some of the ways you can cope with the complex and somewhat mystifying process of large gift fund raising, I'd like to emphasize what I feel is the absolutely essential ingredient—the attitude of those of us whose job it is to secure truly large gifts. I do not believe it is possible to sell anything important or expensive to someone else unless you are completely sold on the product yourself.

My product is Stanford, and I am deeply committed to both its present purpose and its future well-being. If you don't feel the same way about your college or university, you may be in the wrong line of work. But if you do, your prospective donors know it and many will be moved by it. Your loyalty and enthusiasm will be communicated to them so that they will share your feeling that you are inviting them to join in one of life's most rewarding endeavors, participation in a cause greater than oneself.

Good luck!

Chapter 12

The Campaign Case Statement

Richard D. Chamberlain
Vice President, Development and College Relations
Colorado College

T he case statement is perhaps the single most important document of a capital campaign. When you are planning future campaigns, you will find that the case statement provides the best historical perspective as to what this campaign was all about.

The successful case statement will: (1) clearly define and explain the priorities of your institution by capsulizing its hopes and dreams in a believable manner; (2) demonstrate that the values and purposes of your institution and those of your prospects are shared or at least similar; (3) be so compelling that it will move your institution to the top of your prospects' list of philanthropic interests.

Since the case statement is in many ways the culmination of the campaign planning process, you begin to work on it when you begin to assess the needs of your institution. Depending on the size and complexity of your institution, this may be two to three years prior to the public announcement of your campaign. I don't mean that you are actually writing the case statement at that time, but in the planning process you will begin to assemble the important documents and materials that you will need to write the case statement. The actual work should probably begin no later than a year before the announcement of your campaign. But before you can draft the case statement, you must have the final results of your institution's needs assessment. (See Chapter 4.)

Inside or outside?

Who should write and produce the case statement? Does your institution have the talent to do it internally or should you seek outside counsel? If your institution has already had several campaigns, you might decide to do the case statement the way it was done before. Otherwise, you must assess the publications background of your institution and the personnel currently available. When you are evaluating writing talent, bear in mind that writing a case statement is a little different from the writing that normally occurs on most college and university campuses. Since I've gone through this process at two different kinds of institutions in recent years, I must admit that I chose outside counsel in both cases.

At the first institution, a large public university, there was considerable writing talent and publication capability. However, the campaign was the first comprehensive effort in the history of the university, and the resources needed to do it on the outside were available. I decided to use consultants even though many others believed that the writing talent and publication capability on campus were sufficient. My reasons for moving to the outside were similar at the second institution, a small private liberal arts college. This campaign was also the first comprehensive campaign in the history of the institution. In addition, the relatively short publication history of the institution and the limited writing talent available at the time indicated that outside help was needed.

The decision is often not an easy one. You can review your institution's current publications (none of which include a case statement) and then go over a dozen attractive case statements prepared by a firm specializing in that field, but your decision won't be that simple. When you decide to go outside, the message received by your institution's writing and publications staff is not a subtle one.

Going to the outside

If you decide to use a firm specializing in case statements, you are in luck. Only a few firms follow this specialty, and you could count the good ones on the fingers of one hand. You should interview the various firms, just as you would if you were hiring fund-raising counsel. In fact, the task may be easier. The firms you interview can show you numerous samples of their work for other institutions. As is the case with fund-raising counsel, you must consider both the firm and the institutions it has served. And don't neglect to evaluate the "chemistry" between members of your staff and those from the firm who will be working together. Make sure you know who will be assigned to your institution. If your staff can't get along with the person or people, the relationship won't be productive. Ask to see samples of case statements done by the people you will be working with. If these are the least impressive of the many samples you see, ask for someone else.

After interviewing firms, ask for a proposal from the ones you like best. You've already accepted the fact that you'll have to pay more for a case statement done by an outside firm but be sure to examine the proposal carefully. If you don't understand the cost estimates, ask for clarification. Most firms prefer to do the work in stages or phases and will often quote costs in this manner. You should understand the timing of each phase and what it will accomplish. If you are not a publications expert, ask your staff expert to help you go over the quotes for the various phases. It's essential that you know exactly what you are purchasing at each phase or stage of the case statement preparation process.

What will it actually cost to print your statement? The firm cannot estimate this without knowing how long the statement will be, whether it will be black and white, two color or four color, and how many copies you will need. These are not easy questions. In fact it's impossible to specify the exact length of the case statement at this point. Therefore, you should get a number of quotes on different quantities and different lengths. In this way, you will have as clear an understanding of the total cost of the publication as possible at this preliminary stage. The cost of the case statement may well be the largest single identifiable item in your campaign budget. High quality, four-color, 32- to 48-page books are expensive. So plan for this expense when you are putting together your campaign budget.

Once you have decided to "farm out" your case statement, don't assume that you and your institution will play only a minimal role in its actual preparation. Nothing could be farther from the truth. You and your staff will spend many hours meeting with people from the firm to familiarize them with your institution; showing photographers what to shoot; setting up meetings with students, administrators, and faculty; and going over drafts of the case statement. You will wonder at times whether the case statement is actually being done on the outside or whether you and your staff are doing it.

Balance—the case and the campaign

Most case statements devote 50 to 75 percent of the copy to the case. In fact, few of the case statements that have impressed me have devoted as *little* as 50 percent to the case for support. The balance of the statement is devoted to the campaign. In many case statements, these two sections are prepared as if to stand alone. In fact, some institutions actually print the two sections separately, and you may feel that this would be useful for your institution. But I prefer to have both sections in the same publication. While the other method provides flexibility, a single publication gives you certain efficiencies and budgetary savings.

The description of your campaign and how it will accomplish its goals and meet the priorities of your institution is invariably placed at the end of the case statement. The basic components of this section include: (1) a general overview of the campaign and its goals; (2) an outline of the campaign objectives (table of needs); (3) a more detailed description of the various objectives of the campaign; (4) a scale of gifts needed to accomplish the campaign goal; (5) a list of various gift opportunities; (6) a list of volunteer leadership, often including the board of trustees; and (7) the person or office to contact in case there are questions.

The theme

As you review samples of case statements from other institutions, you should be able to identify the central theme of each one. You might select as your theme what your institution has done well historically and continues to excel at and why it is important to continue to improve in this area. The theme might be your institution's service to your community, state, region, and nation. It might be the importance of the liberal arts and how your institution uniquely addresses the role of the liberal arts in today's society. It might be the importance and quality of the teaching at your institution or of the research. Whatever your theme, be sure you communicate it in a concise manner and credibly. We've all read case statements that make exaggerated and unsupported claims for the institution. It's vitally important to keep your credibility.

While you don't want to exaggerate your institution's claims, you don't want to minimize them either. A boilerplate case statement can make the institution sound indistinguishable from all the other colleges or universities of its type and mission. You want to avoid this kind of statement at all costs. While many alumni will receive no other case statements but yours, those with multiple degrees will have something to compare it to. And corporations and foundations see many case statements. You don't want yours to sound like everyone else's. We can't all be the best or in the "top ten" or even in the top several hundred, but each institution has its own unique strengths and specialties, and this must come through in the case statement.

I believe that an alumnus or other supporter who reads the case statement should be able to say, "Yes, this is my institution. Yes, what it has done is important and believable. Yes, what it wants to do is important, understandable, believable, and exciting. Yes, I will help."

If you're lucky, you'll find that the logo for the campaign naturally flows from the process of developing the theme or focus of the case statement.

Other questions: How long? Color? How many?

My answer to "how long?" is simple: long enough to contain the important points of the case and the campaign, but short enough to be read. Case statements range from a dozen pages to four times that number. You should plan the case statement so that it does not have to be read from beginning to end in one sitting. Most readers will pick it up and flip through from back to front to get a "feel" for the piece. Then they'll look at the beginning and perhaps skip to another portion of the statement, coming back later to review the balance.

Most of the best case statements I've seen in recent years have been in four color. This does not mean you can't do an effective case statement in black and white. When you are deciding whether or not to use color, it's important to look at your institution's publications. If several of your publications, especially your alumni magazine, are in color, the decision to go for color might be routine. If you seldom or never produce anything in color, you may need to think twice before deciding on color. Not only is it an added expense, but it may present a "new image" for your institution—one you don't want. If you choose four color, there will always be a few who say, "This looks expensive." (And they'll be right.)

Most institutions can determine print quantity by answering the question, "How many prospects do we have?" While a strong case can be made for sending a case statement to every prospect, think this one through carefully before you order. Do all of your prospects require a comprehensive version of the case statement? Many colleges and universities print the comprehensive version just for their leadership gift prospects. The rest of the prospects receive a less expensive short version.

The case statement process—Four phases

Like any other important publication, the case statement goes through several steps or phases en route to completion. But I would argue that the most important work done on a case statement is that done before you actually put any words on paper.

Phase 1. During this phase, you are developing the theme, the outline, and the design and format of the case statement. Do not go through this stage in a vacuum. Whether you do the case statement in-house or use an outside firm, involvement of key faculty and other volunteers is more important in this phase than in any other.

Involvement can give key faculty and volunteers a sense of participation in the formulation of the case statement. Remember that this publication, perhaps more than any other your institution will produce, needs to represent a consensus. Let these key people have an opportunity to react to the theme and strategy of the statement. I am not suggesting that this be a publication written by committee. But because this document is so important, it must have the support of a representative group of faculty and volunteers.

Once all relevant materials have been reviewed and appropriate faculty, student, and administrative interviews have been held, you can prepare the outline. The outline and layout of the case statement should include a story board to show the flow of the publication. This will lead to presentation boards to show key individuals what the finished product will look like.

Don't rush through Phase 1. Allow time for the proper review of all available material and the sharing of the theme and concept of the statement. An outside firm can play a particularly important role in this review. Although the few firms that specialize in case statements prefer to do the project from start to finish, some will quote a fee for Phase 1 only. If you have the writing and publications skills in-house, this may be the option for you.

Phase 2. Once you and other appropriate individuals have approved Phase 1, it is time to proceed to Phase 2. Although the design and layout will be further refined in this phase, the most important step is the actual writing of the statement. The writing of the case statement should reflect the character and history of your institution, and, above all, it should have credibility. If you are writing it in-house, you can control these important areas. If, however, an outside firm is doing the writing, be sure to spend adequate time with the writer to help him or her understand the character and special qualities of your institution. Otherwise, you may have to do a good deal of heavy editing, if not total rewriting. This is not meant to be a criticism of writers from the outside. But it may be difficult for an outsider to capture your institution's special character by spending a couple of days interviewing faculty and key individuals.

When you read the first draft, you must judge whether it makes you say, "Yes, this is my institution and what I am reading is believable and compelling." Your donors and prospective donors will let you know by their response (or lack of response) whether you've judged correctly.

Allow enough time to distribute the final draft to key individuals for their reactions. I suggest you get their individual reactions. You don't want them to hold a meeting to discuss and dissect your masterpiece. Above all, make sure that faculty members and volunteers who are quoted are properly quoted.

Phase 3. Phase 3 consists of the actual preparation of the statement through mechanical art. If the statement is being done in-house, you'll probably need to involve the publications experts on your staff.

As you finish Phase 2 and begin Phase 3, you need to determine your photography needs. Most institutions do not have an adequate slide library. Either you don't have the right subjects or the slides you do have are out-of-date. Therefore, you will usually need to do new ones. Here again, you have to decide whether to use in-house talent or a free-lance photographer. In either case, do not turn the photographer loose after a few discussions. Describe in detail what you want. Someone who has been involved with the preparation of the case statement should go with the photographer. This is particularly important if you use a free-lancer.

Phase 4. The actual printing takes place in this phase. I won't go into the pitfalls to be avoided during printing—you probably know them all anyway. Suffice it to say that the look and feel of this publication are important enough to justify the fact that it may be the most expensive publication your institution has ever produced, regardless of whether you do it in-house or use an outside consultant. This is why it's so important to find out how much the printing will cost as soon as the design is approved.

If you or your staff supervise the printing, you will have the control over detail that you need. If you are using an outside firm for this purpose, you will probably have to accept some loss of control, and it will generally cost you a certain percentage over the actual cost. In either case, do everything you can to make sure that any errors are printer's errors and not yours.

Shipping is also part of Phase 4. If your case statement is being printed across town, this will be no problem. But if your statement is being done on the outside, do not forget to include the cost of shipping in your budget. Case statements 32 pages long and printed in four colors on high-quality stock are heavy. Shipping thousands of them across the country is not cheap. (And if you think I'm stressing this point because once I forgot to budget for shipping—you're right.)

Effective use

Most colleges and universities either hand-deliver or mail the case statement to a prospective donor prior to a solicitation call. It's always better to mail the case statement before you make the call, so the prospect will have time to review it before you meet face-to-face.

You can also use the case statement, even when it's still in draft form, to solicit leadership gifts prior to the announcement of your campaign. In fact, some believe the case statement serves its main purpose before it's published. Since nucleus fund solicitations usually take place well before the actual publication of the case statement, this may be true. First, second, and third drafts are often very effective in initial leadership gift solicitations. Not only does the prospect see the general content of the case statement, but he or she often provides useful reactions to the draft. This gives the prospect a sense of involvement that should not be underestimated. Therefore, don't wait for the finished product. Use the basic content of the case statement as soon as you have it.

"Yes, I will help." This is the response you want to hear after the prospect has read your institution's case statement. It is proof that your case statement works. May you hear it often!

Chapter 13

The Campaign Plan

W. Moffett Kendrick
Vice President for Development
Furman University

Y ou've established your goals, your constituents believe in them, and your president is ready to go. So you name a campaign chair, select a few committee members, and get started—or so the uninitiated might think.

But if you've been involved in a capital campaign before, you know better. Capital programs can be endangered when planning does not begin early enough. You must have planning and it must begin early and be thorough. It's all too easy to write a plan that covers only those factors dealing with the fund-raising phase. Your plan—and your campaign—should begin with research, cultivation, and internal preparation. And all these things need to happen months, even years, before actual solicitation can begin.

Research data will be essential to the campaign. If you do not have your records on computer, you need to develop a file format to facilitate uniform, systematic data collection on prospective donors.

A saying we have in fund raising is all too true: "Before there can be fund raising, there must be friend raising." You must cultivate the friends of your institution. People base gift decisions on their level of interest and involvement in an enterprise. Well before the fund-raising phase of a capital campaign, an institution should begin to concentrate its communications programs on informing its publics of its goals, building interest, and encouraging philosophic and physical involvement. Communications specialists should embark on a well-planned schedule designed to communicate the goals and objectives that will be the basis of the institution's campaign.

Careful internal preparation in a capital campaign plan accomplishes many important things:

• It brings operating units into the cooperative mode that will be essential as the campaign intensifies in the fund-raising phase.

• It begins the process of conditioning constituencies toward support of institutional goals.

• It sets the stage for the feasibility study.

• It helps keep the president on track.

• It strengthens the budget process and establishes control early on.

• It emphasizes cultivation and research.

• It militates against second-guessing, a perennial campus malady.

• It creates credibility for the chief fund raiser's managerial ability.

A total campaign plan covers what is to be done before and during the actual campaign. Such a plan has two parts: one for precampaign action and one for operating the actual capital program. Here's an example of the first part of the strategy:

> We now have a statement of strategies to give focus over the next 10 to 15 years as we seek to become a college of first rank and to be recognized as such. Administration and faculty must decide what needs to be done in terms of programmatic enhancement, faculty strengthening, services for students, improvement of facilities, and financial enrichment.
>
> This strategic implementation plan then must be analyzed and costs estimated. It will be essential, in presenting our aspirations to constituencies, that the institution be prepared to show precisely what is to be achieved and how, what the costs are, and within what time frame.
>
> We will begin immediately to accelerate and improve our research on alumni, other individuals, businesses, foundations, and other groups. This will include names of principal decision-makers (in the case of businesses and corporations), what personal influences come into play with individuals, likes and dislikes, biases, relationships, past support by amount and designation, gifts to other groups, evidences of close affiliation, patterns and timing of giving, leadership roles accepted or declined over the years, and special activities that may have a bearing on our chances for a gift.
>
> We must conduct our communications program to convey specifically and on a planned schedule the institution's aspirations. This can be done by featuring positive accomplishments of administration, faculty, and students, and relating these acts to cogent parts of the strategic plan. Programs and program opportunities should be presented in such a way as to encourage good feelings about what is being done here and to develop supportive attitudes about the major steps we plan to take. Our plans for meeting the objectives of the strategic statement should be communicated in an exciting, clearly understood fashion. Features, interviews, "think pieces," progress reports, and so on, can do this very well.
>
> Frequency of publication should be stepped up. The tabloid should be published not less than six times a year, preferably 10. The magazine

should be published quarterly. The content of both should be geared toward articulating our aspirations and our efforts toward achieving those aspirations.

An accelerated program of public appearances should be targeted toward alumni groups, civic groups, and other public bodies such as business associations, professional organizations, and the like. People highly qualified and extremely adept at public persuasion should be enlisted for this effort; these include the president, the academic vice president, respected faculty members with pleasing platform manners, key alumni, trustees, and perhaps even parents and other friends.

The theme should be upbeat—"We are on the move, fast becoming known as one of the nation's finest colleges, an institution aware of its capabilities and possibilities, which knows what it needs to do to improve and is working diligently to do just that."

The goal is to get people excited and talking about us, thus helping to enhance our reputation by endorsement and positive attitudes. We also want to promote a strong sense of involvement in our progress.

The intensified research and cultivation just mentioned should begin six months to a year preceding the feasibility study, with the president's image heightened dramatically during that time.

Influence and policy groups during this time should formally agree on implementation of the strategic plan. This consensus then should be incorporated into the public information program.

At the proper moment, the Board of Trustees, with the support of advisory groups, should decide to investigate the feasibility of a capital campaign. A study (market analysis) to determine this will be in order.

The second phase of a campaign plan, the fund-raising stage, is the most critical of all. Given limited resources, limited market, limited leadership (who ever has enough of the right ones?), and limited time, an institution must depend on a well-conceived plan of action. Because all these factors are limited to some degree, efficient application of those we have is essential. This holds true whether the institution is a university of the first rank like Johns Hopkins, a major state university like Michigan, a prestigious women's college like Bryn Mawr, or an excellent liberal arts college like Furman.

Every institution has its own strengths, weaknesses, opportunities, and obstacles. All of these affect a college's operation in normal times, but they come more dramatically into play during a capital campaign. A capital campaign seems to magnify everything. The pace of meetings and donor visits, the pressure of travel in area campaigns, and the demands of meeting volunteer needs are so intense that even routine matters take on monumental proportions. A campaign plan affords an institution's administrative and volunteer teams a way to establish strategies that will emphasize strengths, minimize weaknesses, take advantage of opportunities, and eliminate or overcome obstacles or threats.

The better the plan, the more efficient the use of budget. Some years ago at the conclusion of a campaign, a small college threw away thousands of expensively produced case statements, commemorative brochures, how-to-give pamphlets, fancy pieces on proposed endowed chairs, and other now-useless supplies. The cost of this waste was in five figures. How did this happen? Because the campaign director ran through his bag of tricks—all the things he'd done in other campaigns—without planning how and when—and by whom—the various pieces would be used.

A sound campaign plan provides a disciplined approach to capital fund raising. It lifts a capital campaign from a selling approach to a marketing approach based on targeted strategies. It keeps both staff and volunteers sharply focused on those things important to success. Since about 90 percent of gifts and grants come from approximately 10 percent of the donors, it follows that you should spend 90 percent of your time on 10 percent of the prospects and the rest of the time on everyone else. A good campaign plan focuses on these top prospects.

A good plan reassures key volunteers that the institution knows where it wants to go and how it expects to get there. The plan builds confidence and credibility. It motivates top executives who are accustomed to good planning and staff support. Busy executives like to know what is expected of them, and they like to know what others on the team will do. They are accustomed to that kind of thorough attention in their own businesses. Your president, too, needs to be kept on track; he or she is a busy executive with a premium on each hour. The campaign plan should specify the best use of the president's time.

A campaign plan calls for schedules of committee meetings, public relations moves, publications, printing and distribution, and campaign solicitation target dates. These schedules facilitate budgeting, help prevent overproduction or premature publication of campaign pieces, assist communications staff in timely dissemination of campaign news, and enhance critical public relations moves.

The campaign plan outlines staffing requirements and utilization. By clearly setting forth responsibilities, schedules, and resource allocation, the plan protects staff from undue demands and pressures and creates a spirit of staff-volunteer teamwork.

Usually a campaign plan is written either by the chief development officer with the advice of outside fund-raising counsel or by counsel entirely. Whichever method you use, you should review the plan with key administration and volunteer leadership. This assures full participation and gives those most sympathetic to and deeply involved in the enterprise a chance to spot flaws or omissions.

A campaign plan should cover these basic details:

1. *Patterns for giving.* In his still cogent book on fund raising, the late Harold J. Seymour listed three essentials to remember about patterns for giving (*Designs for Fund-Raising.* New York: McGraw-Hill, 1966, pp. 26-33). First, you should know the difference between a collection and an organized campaign. Second, you should know the essential characteristics of the giving process and the different types of donors. And third, you must realize the importance of setting a quota—translated into a size-of-gifts chart—if enough money is to be raised to achieve campaign goals. This chapter deals with the third point.

According to the "rule of thirds," in a capital campaign one-third of the goal (up to 40 percent) should come from the top 10 gifts, one-third from the next 100 gifts, and the balance from all others.

Gift charts of various colleges almost always exemplify the rule of thirds. In Bryn Mawr's $41-million campaign, the top eight gifts were targeted to produce $16 million, 39 percent of the goal. The next 60 gifts, in the range of $100,000 to $999,999, were to produce $11.75 million, or 29 percent. All other gifts were targeted to provide $13.25 million (32 percent).

Gift charts may be simple or quite detailed, as Figures 9 and 10 show. But they accomplish the same end: They set sights high for administration, campaign leaders, and campaign volunteers. They keep campaign emphasis where it rightly belongs—on the major gifts.

From living donors over five years (capital gifts):

Gift in the range of	Number of gifts needed	Prospects needed		Total goal	Cumulative goal
		Number	Cumulative		
$10,000,000	1	3	3	$10,000,000	$ 10,000,000
$ 5,000,000	3	9	12	$15,000,000	$ 25,000,000
$ 2,500,000	6	18	30	$15,000,000	$ 40,000,000
$ 1,000,000	25	75	105	$25,000,000	$ 65,000,000
$ 500,000	30	90	195	$15,000,000	$ 80,000,000
$ 250,000	50	150	345	$12,500,000	$ 92,500,000
$ 100,000	180	540	885	$18,000,000	$110,500,000
$ 50,000	370	1,110	1,995	$18,500,000	$129,000,000
$ 25,000	540	1,620	3,615	$13,500,000	$142,500,000
From annual giving over five years				$55,000,000	$197,500,000
From bequests over five years				$32,000,000	$220,500,000
From corporations over five years				$18,500,000	$248,000,000
From foundations over five years				$27,000,000	$275,000,000

Figure 9: A Campaign for Princeton:
Table of Gifts Needed To Obtain $275 Million

Gift category	Number of donors required	Amount required
$1,000,000 and up	2	$ 2.5 million
$100,000-1,000,000	20	$ 4.0 million
$10,000 to 100,000	100	$ 2.0 million
Under $10,000	all others	$ 1.5 million
		$10.0 million

Figure 10: The Capital Campaign at Babson College:
Size of Gifts Needed

You must also consider source pattern. Where will the gifts called for in the size-of-gifts chart come from? When you know the principal source of the gifts, you can direct your overall campaign strategy toward that segment of your constituency. This should be clearly set out in the written plan, both as a guide and as an orientation tool for campaign leadership.

2. *Campaign schedule.* In developing a campaign schedule, you should consider: (a) campaign strategies and (b) ongoing permanent fund-raising programs such as annual giving and reunion giving. The schedule may cover a few months or extend over several years if the goal is a heroic one for the institution's size or fund-raising history or because of other factors. Whatever the length, when planning your schedule, you should take the following features into account:

• *Institutional readiness*: Up to two years in advance of campaign announcement, you will need to begin to work toward a consensus about institutional needs that will become campaign goals.

• *Research*: A minimum of two years before announcement, identification of potential major donors and the accumulation of detailed information that will aid in solicitation and in determining campaign leadership potential should begin. Of course, research should be an ongoing part of every development program.

• *Cultivation*: An information program for potential donors and leaders should be in place at least a year in advance of fund raising. Cultivation should involve broad public moves as well as specific efforts aimed at prospective givers, whether individual or organizational.

• *Readiness and feasibility*: You will need a study to determine readiness and feasibility. This should be conducted by a third party, usually a counseling firm, which may or may not be retained for the campaign. This readiness analysis helps the administration identify areas that need attention before the institution is ready for a capital campaign. The feasibility study analyzes constituency reactions to institutional goals and the cost of achieving them. Depending on size, demographics, and other factors, this phase could take three to four months.

• *Leadership recruitment*: This involves recruiting the top person and persuading him or her to make a financial commitment. This sets the stage for the recruitment of everyone else. It takes time to select and involve the kind of person needed to lead a major effort. And he or she will need time to consider the offer of this leading position. The prospective chair must consider the time involved and decide whether the investment of energy and hours can be freely given, and then make plans to delegate corporate or professional duties to associates. Chairing a campaign must not be a half-hearted endeavor. Finally, a chair's first task is to make a gift, so he or she must make the critical decision on the size of the pledge and the payment plan. Since a campaign is never a single-handed effort, the chair must recruit the top core group, obtain their commitment to lead, solicit them, and obtain their financial support.

Recruitment of leadership can take one month or several. It should be accomplished as quickly as possible but not at a sacrifice of thoroughness.

• *Scope*: A campaign aimed at a relatively small number of prospects might be conducted over a few months, a year, or several years. Another campaign group might decide to contact all alumni, no matter how widely dispersed they are. Whatever the scope of your campaign, the schedule must cover the full range, allowing enough time to satisfy campaign demands.

You can use a flow chart to plot campaign actions. Within each major element, list the detailed actions. This leads to efficient use of staff and volunteer time and improves budget control. (See Figure 11 on the next page.)

However detailed the schedule, bear in mind that while tight deadlines keep things moving, be sure to allow a realistic time frame within which volunteers with busy private and professional lives can comfortably perform.

3. *Public relations.* A well-planned campaign contains a well-planned, flexible public relations program. Campaign strategy largely determines the public relations moves that need to be made. Thus, the campaign should map out a general course for communications staff to follow in interpreting campaign goals and objectives to various constituencies. This will involve campus publications as well as electronic and print media. The role of a speaker's bureau might also be covered. The plan should enumerate the campaign documents, their purpose, when they should be released, and to whom they should be sent. Any other activities for cultivation or information should also be spelled out.

4. *Campaign policies.* Well-stated campaign policies can help prevent misunderstandings that lead to warping of campaign goals, loss of pledges, confusion about the role of ongoing programs, and many other problems. Donors need to know what is to be counted in a campaign, what are the dates within which gifts will be credited, what relationship the campaign has to annual giving programs, how pledges will be handled, and so on. Giving and crediting policies form a critical part of any campaign plan and call for their own carefully formulated strategy. Policy statements should be especially designed not only for the institution but for each campaign at the institution.

In a campaign in 1957, for example, Harvard leaders were anxious to prevent an excellent reunion gift program from suffering because of the capital campaign, and vice versa. A policy statement set the matter in focus:

> We are particularly concerned with the relationship of the classes approaching their twenty-fifth reunion when they would normally be raising a large sum of money for presentation at Commencement. An unrestricted gift to the Harvard Fund made from now through June 1959 by members of the Classes of 1932 through 1938 will be credited to their twenty-fifth anniversary gift provided it is understood that, in the case of very large gifts ($10,000 or over), a portion only will be so credited in order not to distort the twenty-fifth year gift.

Babson College covered the subject of gifts to be counted in its 1976 campaign with the following:

> Using October 15, 1976 [the date the Trustees authorized taking steps to move ahead] as the starting date, it is suggested that the following be included in the campaign total:
> • All gifts and pledges negotiated by the campaign organization.

- All unrestricted operating funds (as outlined above).
- Foundation grants.
- Corporate grants.
- Gifts of property, including securities, real estate, life insurance, etc.
- Bequests realized during the campaign period.
- Life income trusts in special situations.
- Government grants for purposes within the program.
- Payments on past capital pledges received after October 15, 1976.

A Furman University trustee, looking ahead to a campaign, began to make gifts in advance to make a more heroic commitment possible. When the campaign began in 1979, the policy on crediting took his foresight into consideration:

> All gifts and pledges made to Furman during the capital period commencing with the official decision of the Board of Trustees to proceed will be credited to the campaign. Certain gifts already have been made to Furman in anticipation of specific goals. Those gifts that are prepaid will be counted.

5. *Scope of organization*. How will the money be raised? How many different donor groups will be solicited, and what kind of organization will be needed? What different income levels will be solicited, and how will they be solicited? The organization structure of the campaign depends largely on the characteristics of the donor base, campaign goals, and the number and sizes of gifts required for success.

A small steering committee is usually established to monitor progress, review results, solve problems, agree on adjustments to the plan, and keep the pressure on the campaign teams. This committee, or another small select group, solicits the top dozen or so prospects. You may also need additional solicitation committees but this will depend on your strategies for groups such as alumni, parents, friends, local firms, local foundations, church or applicable groups, national corporations, and national welfare foundations.

6. *Responsibilities*. The plan should clearly define the responsibilities of chairpersons, committees, administration, and staff. You need to specify exactly what is expected of each person, the relationship of volunteers and staff, and the limits of responsibility of each person or group.

If you decide to use a consultant, the plan should also define the important working relationship between the development staff and outside counsel. Does the consulting contract call for counsel only or will field personnel from the firm be on site to operate the campaign? In a "counsel only" contract, the consultant advises the development staff, which is responsible for campaign management. In a field staff operation, the consulting firm has authority for campaign management. Staff management plays a supportive role with specific but critical responsibilities.

In a counseling-only situation, Furman's plan specified that campaign management would be provided by its vice president for development. His responsibilities included working with counsel's staff "to assure the most effective use of their talents and counsel."

With a full-service contract, the University of Mississippi's campaign was directed by a member of the staff of the counseling firm under contract. This director was to collaborate closely with officials of the university foundation, the administration, and the volunteer leadership. The chief fund-raising executive of the university, like other administrators, was an ex officio member of the steering committee and was to provide liaison between the committee and the university. The vice president of the university foundation, as well as the president, was a member of the steering committee and had a similar liaison capacity.

7. *Campaign budget.* How much a campaign will cost and how it will be financed often plagues institutions. Campaign costs vary widely from about 2 percent of the goal to 8 or 9 percent.

The cost depends on the time it takes to conduct the campaign, the size of gifts, the number of prospects solicited, and the internal costs charged to the budget. For example, a five-year campaign will usually be more costly than a six-month effort. A greater-than-expected number of very large gifts can accelerate success and keep down campaign costs. A campaign confined to a few prime prospects can be more economical than one aimed at a broader constituency; on the other hand, costs can be just as high in such a campaign if creative and expensive activities are necessary. Budgets can also be inflated if the institution's accounting practices dictate that long-range-use items such as furniture, machinery, building modifications, and the like must be charged against the campaign budget. In one such situation, campaign costs were over 7 percent of the goal, but actual expenditures on campaign activities were only 4 percent.

Some institutions allot funds up front, some pay for the campaign from interest earned on unrestricted campaign funds taken in, some budget as they go, and some expect the campaign to pay for itself by exceeding the goal. Whatever your institution's budget process, you must decide in the beginning how to meet campaign expenses. In this way, you can prevent internal misunderstanding and strife among well-intentioned administrators, trustees, and volunteers.

8. *Spatial and mechanical requirements.* A capital campaign requires additional staffing and this means more working space and equipment. You may also need extra storage space, if only for the duration of the campaign.

Campaigns also need vast amounts of information, often quickly. This can place stress on an institution's computer if gift, pledge, and personal data records are computerized. All of these needs and others—automobiles, for example—should be dealt with in the campaign plan.

9. *Support of institutional units.* No less important than space and equipment is the support of other institutional units. By emphasizing the value of supportive units, the campaign plan lays the groundwork for cooperation. You should be as specific as possible about the institutional help you will need. You should specify how often and when you will need campaign reports from the computer center and the development records office, news releases about campaign progress, stories in alumni publications, and so on.

A communications director or a computer center director with a bruised ego cannot kill a campaign, but he or she can certainly make life difficult for the campaign director.

10. *Publications required.* You don't want to produce publications you don't really need or too many copies of a particular brochure or not enough. On the other hand, you don't want to let a key facet go uncovered. Good campaign planning requires that you schedule each publication needed to support cultivation and solicitation strategies and describe its purpose. This not only facilitates the efforts of the volunteers, but also assures them of information support. And it makes it possible for you to determine publication costs to put in the budget.

Conclusion

Capital campaigns, like death and taxes, will always be with us. Only careful planning can guide administrators, staff, and volunteers through the complicated, often discouraging and frustrating journey that is a capital campaign. A sound campaign plan enables you to plan, organize, motivate, and control the people and events that make up your capital campaign effort.

Chapter 14

Capital Campaign Organization

Richard F. Seaman
Vice President for Development and Alumni Affairs
Skidmore College

T he successful generation of capital gifts depends on the development of effective volunteer and staff organizations, for it is they who will jointly identify the capital prospects, cultivate and involve them, solicit them, and provide them with appropriate stewardship.

A word of caution here: Conceptualizing an effective organizational structure for volunteers and staff takes time. It takes even more time to enlist and train volunteers and staff. When you are writing a campaign plan, be sure to allow enough time for these central activities. The success of the campaign depends on them.

Before you can develop the most effective volunteer and staff organizations for your institution, you need to answer the following questions:

1. Have you completed your campaign plan? Does it call for a traditional "every-member-canvass" campaign? Or are you skimming the prospect pool to invite capital gift support from a select audience of prospects on a regionally assigned basis with a specified minimum ask?

2. To what extent is your institution committed to a "volunteer-driven" versus a "staff-driven" solicitation philosophy? Have you really thought through the benefits and consequences of both approaches?

3. How are you going to deal with annual fund and capital gift asks from your best prospects? To what extent are you attracted to the "single ask" theory of fund raising versus the "dual ask"?

4. Seeking capital support is a continuing process whether you are in a campaign mode or not. How do your volunteer and staff organizational structures relate to the needs of the institution during and after a specific campaign?

Your responses to these questions have a major impact on the nature and size of the volunteer and staff organizational structures that can best serve your institution in a capital campaign.

Basic concepts for the volunteer organization

As you contemplate the best volunteer structure for your own institution, consider these key organizational concepts:

1. Your organizational structure starts at the top with your governing board. The board has ultimate fiduciary responsibility for the institution, including fund raising, and it is essential that it be centrally involved at the highest levels throughout any capital gifts effort.

2. The institution's president or chief executive officer inevitably plays a central role in the success of any capital gifts program and therefore must be involved at every stage.

3. Your volunteer structure should enable you to maximize the number of volunteers from every source—alumni, parents, friends, faculty, students, corporations, and foundations. A strong volunteer organization can broaden your program's outreach, develop a larger visibility and a sense of ownership for the capital gifts program, and serve as a means of self-cultivation of capital gift prospects on the theory that the best donors are those who know, care, and work.

4. The volunteer organization should embrace all of the appropriate constituent groups of the institution, including students and faculty. Each constituency has important contributions to make to the overall success of the capital gifts effort.

Central components of a volunteer organization

What are the central components necessary to a sophisticated capital campaign volunteer structure?

The governing board. Primary responsibility for fund raising is always the province of the board of trustees. Typically this responsibility is delegated to one of its working committees, a development committee or resources committee, for example. The board usually issues a mission statement or "charge" to the committee to clarify its duties and responsibilities. The committee commonly focuses on the development and oversight of the broad parameters of policy, rather than on the day-to-day functioning of a specific campaign.

To assure an effective volunteer structure, you must first fully involve the trustees in the campaign. Here are some time-tested ways:

1. Involve the chair of the board with the highest policy committees of the capital campaign.

2. Involve the chair of the development or resources committee with the highest campaign policy councils.

3. If at all possible, select as the national chair someone who is currently active on the board. Appoint your national campaign chair to serve on the development

committee, and have the chair of the board and the president of your institution attend meetings of that committee.

4. Involve as many trustees as possible in the campaign.

5. Establish clear channels of communication between the national campaign chair, the campaign committee (and volunteer organization), the development committee of the board, the president, and the full board of trustees.

The national chair of the campaign. The national campaign chair provides both real and symbolic leadership. It's the most important volunteer appointment you will make. When you recruit a national campaign chair, look for these qualities:

• The chair should be an alumnus of your institution.

• He or she should be a current member of the board of trustees.

• He or she should be able to devote a significant amount of time to the campaign (ideally in the range of 15 to 30 percent).

• He or she should have the confidence and support of the chair of the board and the president.

• Those who will be invited to contribute leadership gifts to the campaign should view the chair as being a person of stature and influence.

• The chair should be capable of making a pacesetting contribution to the campaign to provide the giving leadership essential for success.

• He or she should be an effective leader, both willing and able to enlist and motivate volunteers.

• He or she should be a capable spokesperson, willing to travel and be a focal point for the campaign.

• He or she should be an effective solicitor of pacesetting gifts who enjoys the solicitation role and is able and willing to ask for top gifts.

The campaign committee. The work of the campaign is traditionally done by a number of working committees with specific responsibilities for separate components. This committee serves as the coordinating agency for the campaign and customarily consists of the following people:

• national campaign chair (chair of this committee);

• national major gifts chair;

• regional special gifts chair;

• general gifts chair;

• corporations and foundations chair or chairs (sometimes there are two separate committees);

• planned giving chair;

• annual giving chair; and

• ex officio members—chair of the board of trustees, chair of the development committee of the board, the president of the institution, and the president of the alumni association.

Each committee chair should be a person of stature and influence. For this reason, committee meetings should be planned carefully and held only when needed. Full committees probably need to meet quarterly or semiannually. Some of the operating committees may need to meet every six to eight weeks or more often.

Many institutions appoint a smaller campaign executive committee to resolve any urgent problems or make critical decisions between meetings of the full campaign committee. The members of this committee can be selected from the membership of the full campaign committee, but surely should include: the national campaign chair, the chair of the development committee of the board, the president of the institution, and the chair of the national major gifts committee.

The national major gifts committee. This is perhaps the single most important committee. In most campaigns 80 to 90 percent of the funds come from 10 to 20 percent of the donors. The national major gifts committee has primary responsibility for the identification, cultivation, solicitation, and stewardship of these top prospects.

Each institution will have to determine what level of prospects to assign to the national major gifts committee. A rule-of-thumb is that 10 percent of the constituency will have the capability to contribute in the $10,000-plus range. Thus, in smaller institutions, the national major gifts committee may have responsibility for this level of prospects. At larger institutions, with a larger "floor" of potential support, the committee might handle prospects in the range of $50,000 to $100,000 and over.

The national major gifts committee plays a critical role in the volunteer organization. Its members will manage the institution's top prospects in a nationally oriented approach. In consultation with the campaign's top leaders, they will attempt to comply with the formula for fund-raising success: The best solicitors invite the support of key prospects at the right time and the right place after the prospect has been properly prepared for the solicitation.

Selecting the members of the national major gifts committee is an important step. In addition to the chair of the board, the president, the chair of the development committee of the board, and the campaign chair, the other committee members should meet these criteria:

• The volunteer is capable of contributing at a national major gift prospect level.
• The volunteer is an effective solicitor or is willing to learn effective solicitation methods.
• Major gift prospects perceive the volunteer as an effective institutional and campaign leader.
• The volunteer is willing and able to commit the time to this activity and to complete assignments in a timely fashion.

The regional special gifts committee. Just as the institution's top prospects are handled at the national level, the next level of prospects are traditionally solicited through regional committees. The regional committee chair has responsibility for the identification, selection, training, and supervision of the regional network of committees. These committees are formed in every area where there are enough special gift prospects (for example, 25 prospects to be contacted by a committee of four or five people). A common range of prospect potential for regional committees is $10,000 to $50,000. In smaller institutions, a $5,000 to $25,000 range is common; larger institutions may use a range of $25,000 to $100,000.

The function of regional special gifts committees is similar to that of the national major gifts committee.

General gifts. Should you seek capital gifts from prospects whose potential is no higher than $5,000 over a three-year period? This has long been a subject of debate within the fund-raising profession.

Many argue that prospects at this level belong in the annual fund and should be solicited for campaign support through that means. Others believe that prospects in this range will not reach their full potential through traditional annual giving programs. If these prospects are invited to give specific capital support during the campaign, the institution will gain new donors and the prospects will increase their levels of giving and possibly become regular donors, developing a new relationship with the institution.

You need to determine which strategy is most appropriate to your institution. If you decide to solicit general gifts, here are some ways to do it:

1. A time-tested approach is the general gift campaign, conducted regionally and organized for person-to-person contact. If your institution has not conducted such a solicitation for several years, you may want to select this option for its constituency-building benefits. It can help you identify new prospects, develop a new cadre of volunteers, and encourage more regular donation patterns. At the same time, however, keep in mind that a general gift campaign is very time-consuming and comparatively costly on a per-dollar-raised basis. You need to evaluate the cost-benefit ratios in the context of marginal-dollars-spent versus marginal-dollars-raised. Would you, for example, spend an additional 20 cents if you knew that you could raise an incremental dollar? Consider the multiples!

2. More and more, institutions are using phonathons to raise capital funds. These may be held on or off campus with paid or volunteer callers (alumni, parents, friends, and students). Or the institution may hire a professional firm that specializes in phone campaigns either on the institution's campus or at the firm's headquarters.

3. Some institutions use the mail to solicit capital funds from the general prospect pool. Such efforts are better than nothing, but are surely less effective than soliciting in person or by phone. This kind of campaign often uses a series of mailings.

Corporations and foundations committee. The corporations and foundations committee provides advice and counsel on the development of specific proposals for and approaches to corporations and foundations. For this committee (some institutions may have separate committees), you need people who are involved in the corporate and foundation arena and who can help provide access in the marketing effort.

Planned giving committee. Wise campaign solicitations will emphasize planned gifts—ones that take into account all aspects of the donor's financial situation including income, assets, and estate plans. Most institutions already have a planned giving outreach of some kind, with an emphasis on retained life income gift opportunities, testamentary provisions, and creative gift vehicles. This is usually organized through class representatives who assist in the marketing of planned gifts. Planned giving in a campaign deserves "front and center" attention to help maximize capital support. The marketing plan for the planned gifts program should be fully integrated into the campaign marketing plan.

The annual funds program. While this book deals primarily with capital gifts campaigns, it's important not to neglect your annual fund just because you're in a campaign. The annual fund program should be fully coordinated and integrated with the capital campaign. You must consider jurisdiction over top prospects; timing of solicitations; interface with reunion programs (what counts, who solicits?); and the role of publications and communications programs, to name just a few of the important issues involved.

Staffing for the capital campaign

Paralleling the volunteer structure is a paid staff that functions in direct and close relationship with it. The nature of the institution and the size of the prospect pool will determine in part the size of the staff needed to carry out the capital campaign plan. Staff will be needed to fulfill the following functions:

1. Campaign planning, organization, and oversight.
2. Prospect identification, cultivation, and solicitation of:
   - national major gifts;
   - regional special gifts;
   - general gifts;
   - planned giving; and
   - corporations and foundations.
3. Campaign supports:
   - public relations and publications;
   - writing (publications and proposals);
   - audio-visual supports;
   - prospect research;
   - cultivation and special events;
   - computer systems (records, reports, automated mail, tracking systems, and so on); and
   - stewardship reporting.

The campaign director. Every campaign effort must have one person with specific responsibility for the planning, organization, and conduct of the campaign.

Such oversight begins with the vice president (or equivalent) who has overall responsibility for fund raising, public relations, and alumni affairs (or a combination thereof). The vice president will be involved in all policy discussions and will especially serve as the interface between the fund-raising function and the president and the board of trustees. Customarily, the director of development serves as the named or de facto campaign director under the general supervision of the vice president. He or she has primary responsibility for:

1. developing the campaign plan;
2. recommending volunteer organizational arrangements and identifying potential volunteers;
3. recommending the staff organization and hiring and training the staff;
4. implementing the campaign plan; and
5. serving as coordinator for, and providing staff support to, top volunteer leaders,

especially the national campaign chair and the campaign committee.

The campaign coordinating committee. A campaign coordinating committee within the institution can further ensure coordination of the campaign effort. The committee should consist of the primary staff leaders who have campaign-related responsibilities, especially the members of the communications and public relations staff who will have major roles. Involve them in the highest planning and policy levels, and they will be able to carry out their important responsibilities effectively.

The national major gifts function. The national major gifts program carries with it an extraordinary responsibility because its outcome will so sharply affect the final campaign result. Accordingly, when allocating staff and program resources, many institutions choose to give a high priority to the major gifts and planned giving functions (including national major gifts and regional special gifts).

Each major gift officer on the staff should be responsible for some 200 major gift prospects. This ratio is based on the theory that each staff member should make direct contact (or arrange such contact by others) with each national major gift prospect at least four times each year. Thus, during a 50-week work year, each staff member needs to make 16 prospect contacts a week, an ambitious undertaking.

Each major gift staff officer also has initial responsibility for developing, recommending, and implementing strategies that will culminate in a maximum ask for each prospect under his or her jurisdiction.

Regional special gifts. A staff-to-prospect ratio of 1 to 200 unfortunately cannot be sustained at the regional special gifts level, as desirable as that might be. Rather, you have to consider how many regional campaigns you can conduct in the course of a year, using a large volunteer group for cultivation and solicitation.

If organized effectively and conducted efficiently, regional campaigns can be conducted in two or three areas simultaneously during a 16-week period (three cycles of such campaigns per year). Obviously, the number of prospects in each region (and, thus, the size of the organization to be served) will determine how many areas one staff member can handle. For example, some institutions open a regional office with a staff member in the New York City area for the duration of the campaign.

Should the staff member reside in the region? How accessible the staff member is to volunteers and how effectively he or she assists them are key factors. Thus, many institutions elect to have regional staff members live in the area in which they will be working, especially when that area is large and the regional campaign is fairly complex.

General gifts. Staffing for general gifts depends on the extent to which the institution elects to pursue capital gifts at this level. If you decide to conduct regional personal solicitation, you can "piggyback" general gifts onto the regional special gifts network. However, if general prospects are assigned to regional staff, you must reduce the number of areas assigned to any single staff member. Regional general gift programs are staff- and volunteer-intensive.

Many institutions engage outside consulting firms to conduct phone programs to reach these prospects. When these efforts are for capital support, the contract usually calls for the consultant to provide a resident director to manage the program. If you include that staffing expense, the cost of capital support secured in this way is in the range of 12 to 20 cents per dollar raised.

It may be even more costly for the institution to conduct such a capital-by-phone program through its volunteer network, although there are real constituency-building benefits to this approach. Most institutions simply do not have the in-house professional capability to undertake such a broad and sophisticated effort within time and budget constraints.

Corporations and foundations. Most institutions have at least one officer who is assigned to corporate and foundation solicitation. The larger your institution, the more officers you will need for this area. The corporate and foundation officer must have very special skills; he or she must be a writer, an effective communicator with the academic community, and the chief marketing agent with the corporate and foundation community.

Planned giving. More and more institutions are merging their planned giving and major gift operations. This enables major gifts officers to market more effectively the full range of gift opportunities in the campaign.

At the same time, an institution also needs a planned gifts specialist who is responsible for the organization, planning, and conduct of the planned gifts function, who serves as resident expert and mentor to volunteers and staff, and who coordinates publications, volunteer activities, and marketing outreach. Larger institutions are able to justify a larger staff of experts. Some even employ their own legal staffs.

Campaign support activities. The staff we've discussed so far deal primarily with the identification, cultivation, and solicitation of prospects. But a whole host of support functions are also vital to the success of any campaign. Crucial areas of the campaign that will need support functions include:
- public relations and publications;
- writing (for publications and proposals);
- audio-visual supports;
- prospect research;
- cultivation programs and special events;
- computer systems including prospect records, gifts and pledge recording, personalized mail capability, and prospect tracking systems; and
- stewardship.

A special word of counsel: Allow sufficient time for these support functions to be accomplished. Planning ahead is critical. For example, unless you provide enough lead time for publications (writing, graphics, and so on), they won't be ready when you need them. Coordination with appropriate volunteers and staff should receive high priority.

Set your standards high, for that is what your best prospects expect and deserve. In the end, your volunteers are only as effective as the support functions that enable them to accomplish their pivotal responsibilities. So give your support functions high priority in staffing and resources, and you will see better gift performance.

Conclusion

An effective capital giving program depends on a well-conceived volunteer organization and staff. It is important that both volunteers and staff understand their respective roles and that responsibilities be clearly divided between them.

It takes time to put together a campaign organization, to form committees, to enlist members. You will need to identify and recruit the best volunteers for they will carry the major burden of solicitation. You can't cut corners here so allow plenty of time for this stage.

Give a high priority to the provision of staff, time, and resources to the support functions so essential to the success of the campaign. Solicitors depend on these supports, and so do the results of your campaign.

Chapter 15

The Campaign Budget

Robert B. Rasmussen
Vice President for College Resources
Union College

T he campaign budget is the financial plan through which you acquire and bring to bear the necessary resources to carry out the campaign plan and achieve the campaign objectives. This may sound like a fairly straightforward item. A budget looks so exact with its neatly arranged columns of figures, percentages, dates, totals, and so forth. After all, it is supposed to be derived from a well-documented operational plan. Why then does it merit a whole chapter in this book? And why is it often a subject clouded in the fog of confusion?

The insidious thing about budgets is that they can look so very exact with their neatly arranged columns of figures, percentages, dates, totals, and so forth.

A question we must address early on is just how precise to be in developing a multi-year campaign budget. For all of our sophisticated planning, we all know full well that this planning is based upon sophisticated hunches. It would be foolish and self-deceiving not to recognize this. Furthermore, we all know that serendipity will always be an aspect of our endeavors.

Nevertheless, when the campaign is concluded and the results tallied, you are going to be confronted with the actual results of your efforts. One of the ways in which these efforts will be judged is by a comparison of the campaign results with the costs incurred in achieving them.

Therefore, I urge you to develop your campaign budget in detail and document it thoroughly. State the assumptions on which you've based your figures and include appropriate caveats and options. Having to make assumptions is no excuse for avoiding decisions.

While the campaign budget is something you will be thinking about from the moment the campaign is first considered, the actual development of the budget can only be accomplished in concert with the complete campaign plan. Making up the budget will provide you with an important audit step in which you may find yourself reevaluating the campaign plan. Having to decide how much money you are ready to commit to various activities forces you to concentrate on how important each activity really is.

If you are reading this book, I will assume that:

• You are the director of the campaign being planned for your institution and, as such, are ultimately responsible for all aspects of its planning and execution.

• You have had previous responsibility for the direction of a total ongoing institutional advancement program or for a major component thereof.

• You have responsibility for the direction of your institution's entire ongoing advancement program and the direction of a campaign as an intensified effort to achieve specific and ambitious objectives within a defined time frame.

In short, you are probably a seasoned professional now charged with responsibility for a very major effort.

It may be that at your institution the direction of the ongoing advancement pro gram and direction of the campaign are charges given to two different individuals, of which you are one. If this is the case, the following presentation will be of benefit to you in carrying out your responsibilities and in better understanding those of the person with whom you will be working closely. If none of these scenarios precisely fit your situation, I hope you can adapt the information in this chapter to your own needs.

I can also make some assumptions about your institution: (1) It has an ongoing program in institutional advancement; (2) this program will continue and will be melded into the overall campaign; and (3) the ongoing institutional advancement program will resume after the current campaign and continue until the next one.

As campaign director you are responsible for the campaign budget. We can break this down into three areas: developing the budget, selling the budget, and administering the budget.

This chapter outlines an approach to these tasks, provides some suggestions as to how to go about them, and, I hope, helps you avoid at least the major pitfalls.

The purpose of the budget is simple: It provides the campaign director with the resources to accomplish the task. If you don't get the funds you need to raise the money, you won't raise the money. Most college and university presidents and trustees—at least those trustees who have some active role in the institution's development program—know full well that it takes money to raise money. Colleagues at other institutions have probably told them just how much a capital campaign can cost. If their perceptions are accurate, your job of selling the budget will be that much easier.

Developing the budget: Coming to grips with the task

Rule No. 1: Do not *ever* venture a guess as to what the campaign budget should be until you are ready to do the budget. There will be a lot of speculative numbers and so-called ratios thrown at you. Don't bite, even if some of the numbers you hear sound good. Presidents and trustees have memories that could make an elephant blush, and once your planned campaign has been associated with a budget number, even casually, you have complicated the task of selling the actual budget.

Rule No. 2: Remember that you, the campaign director/manager, are going to be the one to develop the budget and you are going to be responsible for it. You will have masses of material and planning "input" from your staff and others, but the budget is not going to be developed by a committee. It is going to be done by you alone.

Developing the campaign budget is not, of course, the only thing you will have to do alone. Periodically, as you plan the campaign, you are going to need to go off by yourself and think things through. Developing the budget is only one of many planning tasks that require quiet concentration.

Rule No. 3: Don't try to do the campaign budget planning all at once. The campaign budget is an aggregate of the projected costs of the full component of campaign activities. Ultimately it is a summary budget, so do your initial budget planning in components as you develop each part of your campaign. Then, as you meld the campaign components into a cohesive plan, you can meld the budget into a cohesive presentation. This melding will have to be done in concert with a series of decisions about priorities so that the final product is a compromise between the different components and their needs.

Developing the budget: Defining what you are creating

The campaign budget is the financial plan to accomplish stated objectives within a stated time frame. Therefore, you cannot do the budget until you know exactly what the objectives are. This means the basic campaign plan must be outlined and the operational activities articulated in some detail.

The campaign budget is also a supplement to the budget for your institution's ongoing institutional advancement program. I endorse the widespread conviction that the extraordinary expenses associated with a campaign should not be commingled with the regular operating budget. I say this even though, as we will see later, an initial source of operating data for the development of the budget will come from the anticipated costs of the accelerated activity of ongoing programs.

I suggest that you use some general guidelines to review the current level of funding for ongoing activities. I do this with reluctance because there are no universally accepted accounting principles that prescribe how individual institutions record their expenses; and the tables of organization, which affect costs, are variable from institution to institution. The more cohesive the organization is, the better the control of the budget will be. However, this does not mean that we should not try to find common measures. (The continuing efforts of CASE and NACUBO, among others, to derive standards are to be commended.)

The budget for the ongoing institutional advancement program includes funds appropriated on a continuing basis to mount an annual giving program; to present grant proposals to corporations and foundations; to make periodic capital gift proposals to selected individual donors; to conduct an estate affairs program; to sustain the public relations program, alumni publications, and news bureau; and to support the alumni relations program on and off campus.

The total budget for such operations is more often expressed as a percentage of the institution's educational and general (E&G) budget than as a percentage of dollars raised. Given the wide variety of programs and the infinitely varied circumstances under which these programs are conducted, this is the only meaningful way to attempt comparisons. At Union College, a liberal arts institution, our budget for ongoing institutional advancement activities has been fairly consistently in the range of 4 to 7 percent of the E&G budget. These figures will vary for each institution depending on its size and the maturity of its programs. There seems to be somewhat greater efficiency at larger institutions, probably because of the economy of scale, but there are also very small shops that appear to be very cost efficient. Whether or not the cost-efficient organizations are also cost effective is an interesting point, and one that is addressed below.

The campaign budget, by contrast, is most often expressed, for purposes of comparison, as a percentage of the funds to be raised. Let me make two points about the term "funds raised." First, it means the amount of monies raised over and above the amount that would be raised without the campaign. That is, "funds raised" is the amount by which your expected campaign total exceeds the amount you would expect to raise if your institution simply continued in its present ongoing mode for the same period.

Second, what you raise is determined by what you count. The gift-reporting standards created by CASE and NACUBO should be used in your year-by-year forecasts and reports of actual funds received. However, for campaign reporting I suggest that your campaign results should also include pledges that will be paid within a specific period of time after the official end of the campaign period and that were achieved through campaign activity. Each institution will have to decide how to handle this matter, but three-year pledges that extend beyond the official campaign end are common.

To summarize, the campaign budget can be defined as follows:

• It is a supplemental one.

• It is built upon, but should be accounted for separately from, the ongoing advancement budget.

• It is developed to fund a program (the campaign) that is undertaken to achieve specific objectives within a specific time frame.

Developing the budget: Organizing the task

When you approach the campaign budget as a supplemental funding plan, it becomes essential that you have a thorough understanding of:

• your ongoing program and the budget that supports it; and

• the role each of your ongoing activities will play in the overall campaign.

The campaign budget must cover three types of costs, each of which you must carefully analyze. These include:

- *increased costs:* costs of the expanded and intensified activity undertaken in each ongoing area of activity;
- *campaign-specific costs:* costs unique to the campaign as an entity; and
- *related costs:* costs normally borne by other parts of your institution in support of your ongoing operation. These costs must be supplemented during the capital campaign.

Because your campaign budget represents supplemental funding for enhanced activity in so many areas, I strongly suggest that you organize it by type of expenditure with appropriate programmatic elaboration. Then break it down into year-by-year components to encompass the entire period of your planned campaign. Figure 12 (see next page) is a summary of a matrix for presenting the budget. The complete budget would show the total dollar number for each category, not the *a-x* subtotals. You'd keep the subtotals on additional sheets to use for presentations (if necessary) and to use extensively in administrative control.

When you use this type of presentation, you are presenting an anticipated budget for the entire period of the campaign; and you are venturing an anticipated total cost. It's best to express the total in constant dollars (today's). No one can accurately forecast the yearly changes in the inflation rate that will occur over the period of the campaign. With this approach you can make yearly adjustments to reflect the reality of the current economy.

Increased costs. Your campaign plan surely calls for increased activity in all the different "shops" of your institutional advancement program. You can estimate increased costs from data you have for these programs. Let's use the keystone of your institutional advancement effort, the annual fund, as an example. Your campaign is probably a comprehensive one, that is, it calls for accelerated activity to raise more money for annual operating, capital, and endowment purposes. Therefore, you will have an aggregate annual fund total for the term of the campaign that is larger than the sum of the yearly annual fund drives would be.

The increased costs would come from:

- more mail (increased printing and postage);
- more phonathons (more bills, more staff travel, and probably more staff); and
- more personal solicitation (more travel and probably more staff).

You can approach major gifts activity in the same manner. Your campaign plan will have goals for major gifts and at least an outline of a proposed total of gifts. You will also have data on a number of prospects. Furthermore, for major prospects to be approached early in the campaign, you will have at least the outlines of cultivation and solicitation strategies. These should give you a sense of the anticipated cost of this activity. Cost items encompass such things as: staff (as always), special meetings, individual proposal brochures, architect's drawings of buildings, photographs, models, and so on. Complete this review for every component of your ongoing operation, including alumni and public relations areas.

Campaign-specific costs. Campaign-specific costs derive from the plan for the campaign and the methodology through which it will be carried out, such as:

	Year 1 planned	Year 2 planned	Year 3-X planned	Total
Travel	$	$	$	$
a)_____	$	$	$	$
b)_____	$	$	$	$
x)_____	$	$	$	$
Proposals and presentations	$	$	$	$
a)_____	$	$	$	$
b)_____	$	$	$	$
x)_____	$	$	$	$
Program staff	$	$	$	$
a)_____	$	$	$	$
b)_____	$	$	$	$
x)_____	$	$	$	$
Research	$	$	$	$
a)_____	$	$	$	$
b)_____	$	$	$	$
x)_____	$	$	$	$
Publications	$	$	$	$
a)_____	$	$	$	$
b)_____	$	$	$	$
x)_____	$	$	$	$
Graphic presentations	$	$	$	$
a)_____	$	$	$	$
b)_____	$	$	$	$
x)_____	$	$	$	$
Miscellaneous	$	$	$	$
a)_____	$	$	$	$
b)_____	$	$	$	$
x)_____	$	$	$	$
Totals	$	$	$	$

Figure 12: Campaign Costs

These categories are the ones I've used in campaigning. You may have a different and possibly more lengthy list. The definitions of each "user" component (*a* to *x*) should be given in footnotes—annual fund, major gifts, publications, alumni programs, and so on. Supporting documentation should provide summaries in narrative form of the makeup of each component dollar total.

• Campaign counsel. You may elect to use resident campaign counsel or have periodic consulting visits made on an agreed-upon schedule. Whatever method you use, you can easily find out the cost.

• Campaign films and/or other media presentations.

• Campaign special events (such as kickoff dinners). You need to know what these events are, where they will be held, and who will participate.

• General logistics. Office space for additional staff and more telephone lines, typewriters, and furniture are some examples of major items in this category. A myriad of others often appear in the budget as "miscellaneous." Although this item is frustrating to work with, don't overlook it.

Related costs. Increased costs and campaign-specific costs are, to some extent, under your control, but now you must consider the support you expect to receive from other areas of your institution and which, presumably, will be paid for by someone else's budget. Items in this category include:

• Travel expenses for the president and other institutional officers. Perhaps in normal noncampaign times, you get a certain portion of the president's time and his or her office handles necessary travel. But in the campaign you are going to make more demands on the president's time, so you need to know who is going to pay the bills.

• Expenses for volunteers. If you have the "ideal" top-level volunteers, that is, they can and will travel at their own expense, then you can relax and celebrate your good fortune—at least momentarily. But don't assume that what is fine for one level of activity will be fine at another. They may get tired of footing the bill.

• Other institutional logistical support. Most campus service offices budget for an anticipated level of support activity for each area, including yours. Be sure you know what is going to happen when you ask for more.

After you have gathered your budget data, you need to review them with your staff to be sure that everyone is comfortable with the operational plans, procedures, and assumptions upon which they are based. Then it is time to go off by yourself and think the budget through and then organize it and test it.

Once you have done this, you will be able to answer the question I warned you not to answer in the beginning—that is, you will be able to anticipate what the campaign will cost in terms of additional funds needed.

Selling the budget

One of the most challenging aspects of our profession is to determine fund-raising costs for our institutions. If you manage your institution's ongoing advancement program, this task is a familiar one to you. Your expertise in dealing with it will help you sell your campaign budget.

Your personal credibility and the relationships that you have developed with your colleagues will be major factors in gaining their endorsement of the campaign budget. I have found it helpful periodically to air the entire issue with the other officers of the college, encouraging them to express their concerns, and welcoming their questions.

As a preamble to an early campaign budget presentation, I presented a short paper that outlined the problems encountered in determining fund-raising costs. I quote an edited version of this paper, with grateful acknowledgement to H. Sargent Whittier, Jr., vice president for development at St. Lawrence University, from whom I liberally borrowed. (The numbers, however, are mine.)

The Cost of Fund Raising

This is a subject that occupies the attention of the concerned professional and is now, in this era of "accountability," attracting the proper attention of many groups and individuals. Although considerable work is being done on the national level and CASE and NACUBO are jointly developing consistent reporting procedures for both gift income and associated expenditures, the data bases are not yet adequate to provide clear standards.

The problem is further complicated when we attempt to determine what are fund-raising costs. The case could be made that nearly all expenses support fund raising in one way or another. Certainly the catalog and other college publications help. But so, too, and to an even greater extent, does the quality teaching of the faculty. Few, however, would assign faculty salaries to fund-raising costs.

While the problem may be difficult, that's no excuse for not trying. Fund raising has been going on at colleges and universities for a long time and, even without the clear definitions and standards that CASE and NACUBO are now working to develop, enough historical "numbers" do exist to provide some cost guidelines that are helpful over time.

In general, fund-raising costs are included within the context of the total institutional "advancement" budget which includes alumni relations, development, publications, and public relations budgets. Two general guidelines for monitoring the total costs of such activities at colleges like ours are that, over time, the total advancement budget should be approximately 5 percent of the institution's E&G budget and again, over time, 24 to 29 percent of the dollars raised.

In attempting to further define how much of these advancement costs are direct fund-raising costs, we find that the picture remains difficult to clarify. Certainly colleges would engage in alumni relations and public relations programs even if they were not engaged in fund raising. However, it is also true, if impossible to quantify, that colleges would not make the level of expenditures they do in these areas if they were not counted upon to have a real effect on the ability to raise funds.

Within this context it is generally believed that the "direct" costs of college fund raising are bracketed in a range of from 8 to 40 percent of the dollars raised in any given year, and that the long-term "average" for colleges like ours for fund-raising costs is in the 18 to 20 percent range. Our proposed capital campaign budget anticipates that the additional funds raised because of the campaign will have a direct cost range of ±4 percent.

The words "over time" summarize an essential concept in the evaluation of the costs of fund raising. In major campaigns the flow of funds to the college or university does not follow a smooth and rising line. The timing of individual major gifts, for example, follows a sawtooth pattern on a year-by-year basis, and trends become apparent only over a period of time.

This is why I suggest that you anticipate the *total costs* of your campaign when you are developing and presenting the campaign budget. The operational plan for your campaign identifies the year-by-year activities, and this should give you the information necessary to develop an anticipated time line for the flow of gifts. A chart can show this data clearly and will be helpful when you are presenting your proposed campaign budget. You can also use it later, when you do presentations to motivate volunteers and to report on campaign progress to prospects.

You can prepare an overlay of the time line for anticipated flow of gifts to put over the data for the proposed campaign budget. This will vividly illustrate why you must provide for the anticipated costs over the entire period of the campaign.

It's possible that there will be times during your campaign when the costs will be a very high proportion of the gifts received. When you present your budget, it's best to be candid about this with your colleagues and, especially, with your chief budget/finance officer. No one likes to be surprised with information like this, so it's a good idea to prepare them for the possibility of occasional periods of high costs and low gift figures.

At this point, we should consider whether your ongoing budget and your campaign budget should be presented separately, as a package, or both. My answer is both; the package presentation gives the total picture, the separate presentation provides the data for administrative control.

If your campaign is a comprehensive one, the campaign totals will include *all* the funds raised for your institution during that period. Therefore, when you present your anticipated budget, you must address the total costs of your operation, both ongoing and specific to the campaign.

In your planning you determined how you are going to count gifts. The CFAE yearly reports, using standards developed in concert with CASE, give clear definitions and are essentially cash flow numbers. It's best to use these standards in developing your data for the budget presentation and in tracking your actual performance as the campaign unfolds. Your president, colleagues, and trustees, need to know exactly how much real money you expect to raise that can be used to meet the needs of the institution.

Your campaign probably specifies what you will count overall and how you will deal with long-term pledges and estate/bequest commitments. With this policy as a guideline, you can produce a time line of "anticipated commitments" to your campaign as well as one for "actual commitments" to show progress. I doubt if there has ever been a campaign in which the goal reached was made up entirely of fully paid commitments. It's important for campaign budget planning and administration to recognize this fact, quantify it as clearly as you can, and deal with it candidly and early.

Figure 13 on the next page shows a useful format for budget preparation.

Once you have completed this organizational work, you are ready to bring it together in a budget presentation. Marshal your arguments and supporting data and develop your presentation. Here's one way to structure it:

Start with the argument for the campaign itself. If your institution didn't have plans and didn't need resources to accomplish those plans, you would not be undertaking a campaign. So your first argument for a campaign budget is the one given you by your colleagues.

Item one in your presentation is the time line that illustrates the results of your campaign effort year by year.

The second item is the year-by-year breakdown of the total anticipated campaign costs (Figure 12, p. 122). Figure 13 follows.

	Year 1	Year 2	Year 3-X	Total
Ongoing budget	$	$	$	$
Campaign budget	$	$	$	$
Total	$	$	$	$
Gifts anticipated	$	$	$	$
Pledges anticipated	$	$	$	$
Total	$	$	$	$

Figure 13: Campaign Years

Now you need to compare the total projected costs of the campaign and the total return expected in terms of actual cash gifts received (using CASE/NACUBO standards) and long-term commitments (Figure 14). The members of your audience have probably already started doing the arithmetic themselves to come up with the numbers you will now give them, and the impact is likely to be dramatic.

Campaign goal—total commitments	$x,xxx,xxx
Gifts anticipated—during campaign	$x,xxx,xxx
Gifts anticipated—long term	$ xxx,xxx
Campaign costs—total (campaign budget and ongoing budget)	$ xx,xxx
Return on investment—during campaign	x%
Return on investment—long term	x%

Figure 14: Campaign Costs and Results

Commitments anticipated without campaign	$xxx,xxx
Additional commitments with campaign	$xxx,xxx
Campaign projected budget	$ x,xxx
Return on investment—campaign budget	x%

Figure 15: Campaign Impact

Figure 15 can be equally dramatic. It shows what you would raise without a campaign and what you expect to raise with the campaign effort.

What these numbers will be for your institution will determine how you present them. My experience suggests that the return on investment for campaign costs will be quite impressive. Institutions and campaign consultants often use this statistic as a stand-alone number when they talk about the cost effectiveness of their campaigns.

It's more important to be cost effective than to be cost efficient. Your job and mine is to raise dollars. Therefore, it's better to spend $400,000 to raise $1.5 million (26 percent return on investment, net $1.1 million) than $100,000 to raise $1 million (10 percent return on investment, net $.9 million).

Administering the budget

You will have to determine how you and your operating staff are going to "charge off" expenditures to the budgets. I give each operating officer the total budget, "ongoing" and "campaign," for their area for each year and ask them to charge their costs as appropriate. This requires item-by-item judgment. You will have to reconcile the cost appropriations yourself on a monthly basis to be sure that the expenditures are properly tracking the activity undertaken. (You probably do this already.)

In the campaign you are going to have to monitor your expenditures against a long-term plan as well as a year-by-year series of budgets. The "ongoing" operations were consigned to history at the end of each year. In campaigning you are accountable for multi-year expenditures and multi-year objectives. Your campaign budget presentation is the start of a "living" process that continually feeds backward and forward into the conduct of an active enterprise.

Chapter 16

Setting the Campaign Goal

Nelson C. Lees
Director of Resource Development
Massachusetts Institute of Technology

One way to set a campaign goal is to go into your most hallowed quadrangle on a clear, brisk night under a full moon and gently sprinkle some ashes above the grass. Then peer closely at the pattern of the ashes to determine what number they reveal.

Alternatively, there may be an *ex cathedra* determination: You are handed a number by an Important Personage and instructed to achieve it.

Failing either of the above, you will be faced with lots of hard work, imperfect estimates, wildly conflicting opinions, and difficult judgments. Here are some suggestions that may help.

The principal ingredients

1. *Your institution's past experience.* If you're planning to do much better than in the recent past, be sure you have good reasons for believing you can.

2. *Your institution's identified potential.* Probably no one ever goes into a campaign with *all* the needed potential identified, but if you have not identified a substantial portion of it, be sure you have good reasons to be confident about coming up with the balance.

3. *The effectiveness of your institution's campaign organization.* All the potential in the world won't do you any good unless you are—or are going to be—organized to go after it effectively.

Evaluating the past

You can't make sound judgments about the future until you have analyzed the past experience at your institution. This should include a careful evaluation of:
- total support over the past 10, and preferably 20, years;
- support by donor type over at least the past 10 years: How has giving by alumni, friends, foundations, corporations, and bequests varied, and are there trends that you can perceive and understand?
- support by purpose: What has been happening to giving for endowment, unrestricted, facilities, programs, and the annual fund?
- support by gift size: What has been happening to giving at various dollar levels (e.g., $1 million plus, $500,000 to $1 million, $100,000 to $500,000, and so on down the scale)?
- recent campaigns: What happened to the categories above as a result of any campaigns you have had over the past decade or so—and do you understand why?

The way to look at these factors is to dig out the data and plot them. Be sure you differentiate significant ad hoc actions—a large bequest, an unusual gift for a building—from trends. It will help if you plot dollars received against numbers of donors by categories.

All of your ongoing dollar data will probably be in the form of cash flow. Always keep in mind that campaigns typically count commitments, many of which are often paid over several years. Trying to relate commitments to cash flow is one of the most nettlesome aspects of setting a campaign goal. A $100,000 entry in the cash flow column may well represent a $500,000-over-five-years entry in the commitment column.

Sometimes you can make rough approximations that are helpful in assessing a proposed goal: For a typical five-year "count everything" campaign, the *eventual* cash receipts will probably include: (1) at least a year of cash flow prior to the formal announcement (nucleus fund); (2) five years of cash flow during the campaign; and (3) the equivalent of another year or two of cash flow after the campaign ends, as pledge payments come in.

If you have 75 percent of your reported campaign total in hand by the end of the formal campaign period, you are doing reasonably well. The remaining 25 percent—invariably including some amount of "bad debt"—will probably come in over a longer period of time, especially if you have included at face value such instruments as charitable remainder unitrusts and pooled income funds (there are arguments for and against doing this). This extended pay-in *might* be equivalent to another two years' cash flow. So the campaign total may have some relation to your cash flow projections over a period of roughly eight years. If you are expecting one or more mega-gifts, obviously these should be factored in.

Improving on the past

"Past is prologue" but that's no guarantee that an understanding of the past will give you insight into the future. Nevertheless, as you look at what your institution has done over the past decade—bearing in mind the ruinous inflation of the late '70s and early '80s, bull and bear markets, and actual and proposed tax code revisions—consider whether your campaign will be able to do 20 percent, 30 percent, or perhaps even 50 percent better than in the past. Your reasons for this optimism might include:

- more and better prospects;
- more, and more effective, solicitors;
- a better "case" for your institution to put to your constituency;
- an expanded and/or strengthened fund-raising organization;
- an institutional commitment to give the campaign top priority, which means, among other things, more time from your president, top academic officers, trustees, and others;
- well-defined specific funding objectives that facilitate the matchup between prospect and project and increase the likelihood of a gift;
- effective stewardship over the past several years with your important donors; and
- better cultivation and involvement of your best prospects over the past several years.

Identifying your potential—the gift table

How do you convert analysis into the "magic number"—your specific campaign goal? You make a gift table, which is probably the single most critical element in determining the campaign goal, and the gift table enables you to compare your need with your identified potential.

What *is* a gift table? It is a projection of how many gifts of varying sizes you will probably need to achieve a specific funding objective. The sizes of gifts on the gift table should be realistic for your institution and your constituency. Figure 16 shows a gift table for a fully endowed $1.5-million professorship for which you believe you can attract multiple donors.

Dollar range of commitments (including pledges, not just cash flow)	Number of donors needed	Projected total commitments
$500,000 plus	1	$500,000
$100,000-500,000	2	300,000
$50,000-100,000	5	300,000
$10,000-50,000	10	200,000
Under $10,000	200	200,000
		$1.5 million

Figure 16: Gift Table

Although the gift table assumes fairly widespread participation among your constituency, it suggests that the chair will be established *only* if you get a comparatively small number of very large gifts. These are your "enabling commitments." You should always solicit the top level of the gift table first. And if you do not know who is likely to make these gifts—that is, you do not have a solid major prospect list—you probably are not going to succeed in funding the endowed chair.

The role of gift tables

Please note the plural. It is relevant in several ways. Once you begin to consider some actual numbers for your goal—$125 million, $150 million, or possibly $175 million—you can develop two sets of gift tables that should converge.

Goal tables. Develop gift tables for each of the different goals to analyze what you would need to achieve them. Unless very unusual circumstances are involved, you will quickly discover that as you move to the larger goals, the burden rests almost exclusively on major donors. It is unlikely you will bring in enough donors in the lower ranges to make up the difference between the lower and higher goals. Nor will you be able to upgrade a sufficiently large number of donors from, say, the $10,000 range to the $100,000 range to make up for the larger total. You need to identify more major prospects if you are going to try for the larger total.

The gift base. When constructing gift tables, you may want to use the concept of a "gift base." At the upper ranges of the gift tables, you have comparatively small numbers of large prospects—perhaps a few dozen, perhaps a few hundred—and you can specify how many such prospects you have, who they are, and what you hope each will do. Below this upper level—a convenient breaking point is $100,000 or $50,000 or $25,000—you'll probably have too many prospects to assess individually in a gift table. You might want to project anticipated cash and/or commitment flow at different levels of solicitation and for different categories such as alumni, friends, foundations, and corporations. This projection, as opposed to the individual assessment of specific prospects, provides a gift base.

A problem in gift tables—and elsewhere in the campaign—is how to handle personal foundations, those that are really extensions of individuals. Do you consider them as individuals or as foundations? There are pros and cons to either method.

Potential tables. Now reality confronts desire. Once you have put together your list of top campaign prospects and decided what each can be asked to consider, list them by decreasing totals. If possible, include the particular proposal or purpose to be made in the solicitation, as in Figure 17.

Tabulate this list as numbers of prospects and total asking amounts by range, as in Figure 18.

Then compare this to what you will need according to your goal tables (see Figure 19). In this example, the top range looks thin but the second range looks strong.

Now you start to see what your overall potential looks like. You are also projecting numbers of donors from numbers of prospects. At this point, it's important that

Mr. Green	$1,000,000	Professorship in art history or literature
Mrs. Brown	$750,000	Student aid fund for the Chicago area
White Corporation	$750,000	Named hall in the chemistry building
Black Foundation	$500,000	Program in health care

Figure 17: Potential Table

Range	Prospects	Asking amounts
$1 million plus	15	$20 million
$500,000-$1 million	20	$14.5 million
etc.		

Figure 18: Potential Identified as of September 1

Range	Prospects identified	Asking amounts	Donors needed	Commitments needed
$1 million	9	$12.0 million	10	$15 million
$500,000	20	$14.5 million	10	$ 7 million
etc.				

Figure 19: Goal Table

you have confidence in your prospects and have rigorously differentiated prospects from suspects.

In the upper ranges of a gift table, the conversion rate might be two or three to one (and in the middle ranges perhaps more)—that is, out of two or three identified prospects, you may get one donor. It is highly unlikely, as you agree on a campaign goal, that you will have identified the full potential that you need. But what's important here is the number of major prospects you've identified. If that number is disconcertingly low, then your proposed goal is probably too high.

It's a good idea to develop tables for foundations and corporations as well as individuals. If you are planning to count realized bequests, use a line item for them and don't try to build them into the gift range tables. The three tables can then be evaluated independently and merged into a composite table.

You also need to decide whether your definition of a donor's commitments means separate actions during the course of the campaign (so the same donor making several gifts would show up in the table several times) or cumulative ones. The latter is more often the case, so that the number of commitments in a given range frequently represents a much larger number of total gift actions over the period. This, of course, means more solicitations.

The cascade and multiple solicitation effects

When you ask prospects in your gift range table for a gift, some will say "no" and disappear as prospects (at least for the time being). Others will say "no" at the range you hoped for—$100,000 for example—but respond with a gift at a lower range, perhaps $25,000 or $50,000.

As the campaign proceeds, more and more prospects at higher ranges will show up as donors at lower ranges. While this may be hard to quantify, bear it in mind when evaluating your gift table.

Conversely, if your table is based on total gifts per donor rather than on separate gifts, you are likely to find that many of the projected commitments in the upper ranges will end up representing two or three or more separate gift actions, each of which will probably require at least one solicitation. So the amount of solicitation it will require to get the commitments you need may be much higher than it appears in your gift table.

Gift range tables in operation

Let's look at some examples of gift range tables for MIT's last campaign (1975-1980). We developed tables for living individuals, foundations, and corporations. Figure 20 shows the final projections before the campaign began:

Range	Living individuals		Foundations		Corporations	
	Donors	Dollars	Donors	Dollars	Donors	Dollars
$5 million plus	5	35-40	4	20-22	0	0
$1 to 5 million	10	12-20	10	15-20	8	9-12
$500,000 to $1 million	10	6-18	12	7-10	12	7-9
$100,000 to $500,000	60	10-15	50	9-15	100	16-20
Total	85	72	76	60	120	37
Gift base (less than $100,000)		22		5		9
Totals		94		65		46

Figure 20: MIT Leadership Campaign:
Projected Sources of Funds (Millions of Dollars)

Figures 18, 19, and 20 project ranges of dollars anticipated for each gift level. This is helpful if you are not confident about what the average commitment size will be within each level. You can then calculate averages from the projections.

We put the tables for all sources together and added a one-line projection for estimated realized bequests during the campaign period. This is shown in Figure 21.

Range	Donors	Dollars
$5 million plus	9	59
$1 to 5 million	28	44
$500,000 to $1 million	34	23
$100,000 to $500,000	210	43
Total	281	169
Gift base (less than $100,000)		36
All bequests		20
Total		225

Figure 21: MIT Leadership Campaign:
Projected Sources of Funds (Composite)
(Millions of Dollars)

That was what we projected as we entered the campaign. More than five years later, when it was all over and we looked back, how well did we do?

As Figure 22 shows, the lower and middle levels of the tables were fairly accurate:

Range	Projected		Actual		Difference
	Donors	Dollars	Donors	Dollars	Dollars
$500,000 to $1 million	34	23	34	22.4	−0.6
$100,000 to $500,000	210	43	219	42.4	−0.6
Total	244	66	253	64.8	−1.2
Gift base (less than $100,000)	n/a	36	n/a	39.3	+3.3
All bequests		20		20.1	+0.1

Figure 22: MIT Leadership Campaign Results
(Millions of Dollars)

The $1 million to $5 million level was far stronger than anticipated. We projected that 28 donors would give $44 million and, in fact, 45 donors gave $83 million.

This was fortunate, because the top level—$5 million and above—was weaker than we had anticipated. We'd hoped for nine donors who would give $59 million and, instead, we got $43 million from six donors.

Figure 23 shows the results when we put all the levels together.

| | All Sources | | | | |
| | Projected | | Actual | | Difference |
Range	Donors	Dollars	Donors	Dollars	Dollars
$5 million plus	9	59	6	43.0	− 16.0
$1 to 5 million	28	44	45	83.0	+ 39.0
$500,000 to $1 million	34	23	34	22.4	− 0.6
$100,000 to $500,000	210	43	219	42.4	− 0.6
Total	281	169	304	190.8	+ 21.8
Gift base (less than $100,000)		36		39.3	+ 3.3
All bequests		20		20.1	+ 0.1
Totals		225		250.2	+ 25.2

Figure 23: MIT Leadership Campaign Results (Composite)
(Millions of Dollars)

Even though the composite table was fairly accurate for approximately 50 percent of the money that came in commitments of less than $1 million and in bequests, there were wide variations in all ranges of the separate tables for individuals, foundations, and corporations. These averaged out in the composite table.

Our experience here was not unusual. Campaign planners often project too many commitments of $5 million and up and too few of $1 million to $2 million. Perhaps planners hope that projections calling for several very large commitments act as sight-raisers, or perhaps they are just too optimistic about what top prospects will actually do.

The gift range table has three roles:

• As you plan your campaign, it helps you see what you will need, and when you compare this with your identified potential, you can determine whether you have a reasonable chance of success.

• During your drive, the gift range table may function as a sight-raiser by defining the number of large gifts needed and encouraging your better prospects to stretch for them; otherwise I don't believe it has much operational use once the campaign is underway.

• After your drive, the gift range table may help you evaluate your constituencies, providing insight for postcampaign fund raising and your next drive.

Any campaign goal has to be a compromise between what the institution needs and what it can realistically hope to raise. One of the most sensitive aspects of campaign planning is the conversion of the institutional wish list into the actual campaign priorities that will make up the overall goal. The priorities list is also a compromise, and it must reconcile priorities that are of central importance to the institution—such as endowment, unrestricted gifts, and critical facilities—with those that are less than crucial to the entire institution but are extremely important to particular schools and departments.

This process can also help focus attention on sustaining priorities that will help existing programs (chairs, student aid, and so on), as opposed to those that are incremental, representing new efforts. We all know that rarely, if ever, are *all* a campaign's priorities fully funded. One of the tactical problems in campaigning is keeping appropriate emphasis on those priorities that are the institution's *real* core needs.

Recapitulation

How, then, is the goal set?

You plot past experience and draw some lines representing various degrees of improvement over what you have been doing, converting cash flow to campaign commitments. You compare these, if possible, with improvement produced by previous campaigns.

You add up your needs, whittle the list down, and see if this rock-bottom minimum looks like it would make a campaign worthwhile.

You tabulate all the potential larger prospects you can identify and estimate a total for their campaign commitments, adding estimates for total gifts by smaller prospects. If you plan to undertake a feasibility study, now is the time.

From the data developed above, generate some possible rough goals—perhaps three or four—for each of which you develop a gift range table. As planning proceeds, you compare these tables with tables tabulating your identifed potential. Slowly a sense of what looks achievable will emerge.

Another substantial factor in setting the goal is what various senior officers of your institution, trustees, and/or key volunteers *think* it ought to be. Their conviction that a certain goal "feels" right may play a powerful role, sometimes conflicting with analysis and evaluation, in the determination of the final number.

What is a "successful" campaign?

I believe a campaign has three levels of success, and that we should keep these in mind when we are planning and setting the goal.

• *Exceeding the goal.* There is a much stronger feeling of success for all who have worked in your campaign when you exceed the overall goal rather than just

137

making it. (This also eliminates any suspicion that you had to manipulate numbers in order to claim victory.) It's like receiving more than 50.1 percent of the vote in an election. So try to plan a goal you think you may be able to go over by a modest amount. Recent campaigning experience indicates that goals are often being exceeded, sometimes to an almost embarrassing extent. So don't set your goal *too* low.

• *Funding the critical priorities.* If you exceed your goal but fail to fund the critical priorities, your campaign did not succeed.

• *Altering the nature of the institution's ongoing gift support.* The final level of success for a campaign is not only increasing the total gifts to your institution each year and making it possible to sustain the higher level, but ensuring that a higher percentage of the money goes to crucial institutional needs, particularly endowment and unrestricted purposes. A further element of success is if you alter the donor composition so that a particular constituency—such as alumni, friends, or corporations—is providing an increased portion of your ongoing gift support.

Envoi

Don't make the mistake of putting more emphasis on the overall goal than on the individual priorities that make it up. When we go from normal fund raising to campaign fund raising, we often suffer significant, and not always recognized, changes in mindset from "Where do we go to fund Building X or Professorship Y?" to "Where do we go for the biggest gifts?" Concern over meeting (and exceeding) the overall goal can blunt the emphasis that ought to be put on the critical priorities that will result in sounder basic finances for the institution.

The word "goal" comes from the Middle English *gol* which meant "boundary" or "limit," and that, in turn, derived from the Old English *gál* which meant "obstacle." Ironically, the word "goal" may be regaining its ancient meaning when our campaign goals become obstacles to what we really ought to accomplish.

Chapter 17

The Campaign Calendar

F. Mark Whittaker
Vice President for College Relations
Sweet Briar College

Begin at the beginning...and go on till you come to the end: then stop.
—Alice's Adventures in Wonderland

The King's order to the White Rabbit is one way to describe a campaign calendar. But unfortunately it's not that simple. When you are planning a campaign calendar, you can't just begin at the beginning. In the first place, several preliminary steps are necessary before you even get to the beginning, such as:

- preparation of the internal audit of needs;
- testing the "case" for the campaign;
- selecting fund-raising counsel (if necessary); and
- recruiting the necessary leadership to reach desired goals.

The amount of time and energy that go into these preliminary steps will depend on the complexity of the organization and the amount of planning required to produce a definition of capital needs. After this, prospect research must be done, top prospects must be evaluated, and volunteers enlisted. Only then can you "begin at the beginning."

Whether you are running a continuous capital fund program or a one-time capital drive, you will need to develop a realistic timetable that takes into account available staff and volunteers. In addition, sound campaign practice dictates that you seek the largest gifts first, and you should plan the campaign calendar with this in mind. Premature solicitation can lower sights and even result in an unsuccessful campaign. Many are the horror stories of the major prospects who gave too little too early.

Plan your calendar on the principle of working from the top prospect down, and remember that the bigger the prospect, the longer the time required for a decision. Identify top prospects at the beginning of the campaign, so there will be plenty of time for cultivation and solicitation. When new prospects are identified during the campaign, you can schedule cultivation and solicitation as appropriate.

Although you may not publish your time schedule for general view, it will probably be quite a complicated document. A major campaign usually represents a collection of individual campaigns, each with its own leadership and time schedules. Once you have completed the campaign calendar, its schedules should be followed, even though circumstances beyond your control may make adjustments necessary.

While the length of a capital fund-raising effort depends on many factors, three to five years is usually the optimum time needed to meet the specific needs of the program. It is difficult to keep an intense capital effort going for longer than five years. Even for that period, it's important to keep the campaign objectives in sight in order to maintain momentum.

Here are some general rules for planning a calendar for a traditional one-time capital campaign:

• Allow one year for strategic planning, review of institutional mission, and development of campaign strategies.

• Program a period of nine to 12 months between the decision to begin the campaign and the actual public announcement.

• Plan on at least one year for major or leadership gift solicitation.

• Begin the every-member canvass or second-level gift solicitation 12 to 18 months after the kickoff.

• Continue both major gift solicitations and second-level solicitations until the end of the program.

Research shows an average of 30 to 36 months from the public announcement of the campaign to its successful conclusion, and four to five years from beginning the initial planning process to the successful conclusion of the program. The general solicitation period should be as brief as possible and should always come at the end of the campaign.

Strategic planning

Let's break down the development of the campaign calendar into manageable sections. First, you will need a calendar for early stages of strategic planning; this is a schedule for discussions with faculty, staff, and administration and for meetings with the board and with major prospects. Be sure to arrange these meetings with faculty and other key institutional personnel so that they don't conflict with the academic calendar. A strategic planning schedule might be as follows:

• initial meetings with faculty, staff, and students (two months);

• the development of a strategic planning discussion outline (one month);

• board of trustees and prospect discussion of the strategic plan (six months or three meetings); and

• final recommendations and conclusions to be used in the development of the case statement.

Case statement calendar

Once you have gone through the strategic planning process, you should develop a schedule for preparation of the case statement. The essential element of the case statement is the mission of the institution. This should clearly state the central concerns of the organization. Here the schedule calls for determining dollar estimates for specific goals. You will need to review this information with the administration and develop strategies for the effective solicitation of top prospects. It takes time to identify those individuals who will specifically benefit from the capital campaign objectives. Preparation of the case statement must involve key staff, trustees, and volunteers, as well as major donors. Development of the case statement is one of the most important steps in preparing for a capital campaign. The writing of a case statement may take several months, and it may go through numerous drafts.

Feasibility study calendar

The length of time a feasibility study takes depends upon the number of interviews and the geographic distribution of those to be seen. If an outside fund-raising consultant does the study, you may need two to three months to select one unless your institution has used counsel before and plans to use the same firm. Many institutions interview three to five firms before making a decision, and this process inevitably takes time.

Once you've selected counsel, an optimum schedule will call for four to five interviews a day, if those to be seen live near one another. If extensive travel is involved, two interviews a day might be a minimum. Again, the time required to complete a feasibility study depends on the number of people being interviewed, where they live, and how many members of the consulting staff are interviewing. Only a careful analysis of these factors will make it possible for you to plan the feasibility study calendar.

Assessing internal readiness

The success of your capital campaign depends in large measure on the institutional resources within the advancement or development organization. In preparation for the campaign, you should undertake an internal audit, preparing job descriptions for all members of the staff and developing a staff organization chart and a comprehensive campaign fund-raising plan. You need to analyze how annual giving, planned giving, and support from foundations, corporations, and government fit into the overall program for the solicitation of major gifts.

You or your research staff must collect and analyze detailed biographical information on the trustees and other top volunteers who will be making calls. You need to review the strengths and weaknesses of the volunteer organization and get from every volunteer a commitment to raise money for the institution.

How well do you know your top prospects? The ability to begin the capital campaign depends on your knowledge of these major prospects. You need to develop a prospect giving chart. There are several types of rating systems you can use to select top prospects. The time this takes depends upon the amount of research already in place and the kinds of records available. If your institution has a computer record system and has maintained biographical files, you ought to be able to come up with a suspect list fairly quickly. The next step is to select those individuals who are in the best position to give advice on the potential of the suspects and to identify those who might give leadership gifts. (Of course they can't do this until you have defined "major" or "leadership" gift for the purposes of this campaign.)

Three to six months should be sufficient for the initial review of the prospect list and determination of potential and probability ratings for these individuals. You'll need more time for this stage if rating sessions are necessary to give research and in-house records more detailed analysis. Some institutions take a year for intense research in key geographical areas and interviews with volunteers to identify and rank top prospects.

If field work is required, allow time so that you can select meeting locations and identify the best sources of information (alumni, parents, and trustees) in those areas. Someone must interview these knowledgeable sources. This kind of prospect research enables you to prepare a campaign calendar that clearly illustrates the principle of working from the top prospects down—beginning with the solicitation of trustees and top volunteers.

You should ask the president, top administrators, and volunteers how many days they are willing to give for solicitation of major gift prospects. Make a list of trained solicitors and try to determine how long it will take to bring them up to speed in the solicitation of major gifts.

Again, there are no formulas to specify how long each step of preparation should take. Much depends upon the professional expertise of the advancement organization and the leadership ability of the top administrative staff. In short, the development of the campaign calendar requires a realistic assessment of the time needed for strategic planning, development of the case statement, selection and use of fund-raising counsel, and internal preparation.

You can structure the calendar for the actual campaign either in phases or by year, whichever is most useful to your institution. A phase calendar allows for more flexibility in adjusting specific schedules. On the other hand, if you use a year-by-year model, it is easier to assign dates and allocate time. The phase model shown below was initially developed by Jack Butler, President of Barnes and Roche. A version of it also appears in M. Jane Williams' book *Capital Ideas*, published by the Fund-Raising Institute in Ambler, Pennsylvania. There are seven phases:

Phase 1: Planning

- Complete long-range institutional planning.
- Conduct the internal survey of alumni, parent, and friend constituencies.
- Prepare the case statement.
- Determine the role of professional counsel and select and hire counsel, if needed.
- Analyze annual giving, planned giving, and foundation and corporate support programs. Strengthen each program as much as possible.

Phase 2: Organization

- Establish campaign priorities and objectives.
- Enlist key leadership starting from the top.
- Prepare campaign materials, including the case statement, subscription forms, opportunity booklets, and individual capital project brochures.
- Start cultivation programs for major gift prospects.
- Solicit the board.

Phase 3: Campaign work begins

- Obtain final approval of the program.
- Complete the enlistment of volunteers.
- Complete the development of a rated prospect list.
- Complete the hiring of any additional development staff.
- Set the final campaign goal.
- Continue cultivation programs for the top prospects.
- Begin the distribution of materials to top volunteers.
- Conduct solicitation training sessions for top volunteers.
- Solicit top prospects.

Phase 4: Big gift stage

- Assign top prospects to solicitors.
- Prepare for solicitation of second-level prospects.
- Plan for constituency-wide solicitation of all alumni, parents, and friends.
- Establish a regular reporting system on the progress of the capital campaign.
- Circulate progress reports.

Phase 5: The campaign in high gear

- Take all necessary actions so that solicitors are active.
- Complete the solicitation of all major gift prospects.
- Continue to distribute campaign reports to the volunteers.
- Continue cultivation activities.
- Conduct every-member solicitation campaigns.
- Continue reports in stewardship to volunteers and donors.
- Consider final reporting activities.

Phase 6: An orderly conclusion
- Analyze the campaign efforts and impact on the institution.
- Acknowledge participation by volunteers and major donors.
- Wrap up all campaign operations.
- Begin resurveying of the donor constituencies in terms of level of support versus prospect ratings.
- Continue cultivation activities of top prospects.
- Distribute the final campaign report.

Phase 7: Start all over again

Capital Ideas also includes a year-by-year model written by Russell V. Kohr for *Handbook of Institutional Advancement* (A. Westley Rowland, gen. ed., San Francisco: Jossey-Bass, 1977, pp. 236-264). Mr. Kohr is coordinator of capital programs at the Ravinia Institute for Young Artists in Chicago. A variation of this calendar is as follows:

First year:
- Complete first draft of the long-range plan (involves administration, faculty, staff, trustees, selected volunteers, and so on).
- Share the institutional plan with trustees and selected major gift prospects.
- Revise the plan as necessary.
- Secure trustee approval of the plan and the campaign goals.
- Prepare gift opportunity statements.
- Draft the case statement and share it with key persons in the organization, trustees, and other top volunteers and prospects.
- Survey various constituencies.
- Research prospective donors for major gifts in all constituencies.
- Begin solicitation of major gift corporate and foundation prospects.
- Increase annual gift solicitation.
- Enlist a national campaign chair and chairs of major gift committees beginning with the president, chair of the board of trustees, and the chairs of the various trustee committees.
- Define the role of the president and other administrative officers.
- Begin solicitation of trustees.

Second year:
- Distribute campaign case statement to national campaign leadership and key prospects.
- Begin solicitation of key prospects.
- Enlarge staff as necessary.
- Plan the major campaign kickoff and other special events.
- Continue research on prospects for special gifts.
- Enlist and train volunteers who will solicit special prospects.
- Begin solicitation of special gift prospects.
- Organize and hold status report meetings.

Third year:
- Continue all phases of major and special gift solicitation.
- Complete all research on top prospects and research of prospects for the general campaign.
- Enlist volunteers for the general campaign.

Fourth year:
- Distribute the case statement to prospects for the general campaign.
- Organize and conduct local area campaigns.
- Organize and conduct regional campaigns.
- Schedule report meetings and public events.

Fifth year:
- Consider plans for postcampaign fund raising, including continuing emphasis on annual giving.
- Complete local and regional campaigns.
- Arrange and implement the final campaign celebration.

Whether you use the phase or the year-by-year model for your calendar, you will need to develop schedules for specific tasks. The overall campaign calendar has to include time projections on recruitment and training of volunteers, research of prospects, and so on. Figure 24 is a monthly schedule.

Campaign activity	January	February	March
	(Assign staff and date for each month)		
Draft case statement	Mark 1/15		
Plan trustee meeting	Mary 1/17		
Recruit solicitors	Jack 1/18		
Prepare printed materials		Mary 2/21	
Survey constituencies			Jack 3/2

Figure 24: Sample Monthly Planning Chart

Sometimes it helps if you plan the campaign schedule backwards. For example, begin with the date the campaign is to end and schedule activities back from that point. This method is often used for planning celebrations of anniversaries or major changes in direction.

Many campaign activities have to happen at the same time throughout the program. There are also certain times when the institution must focus on one specific activity, such as the solicitation of the board and top prospects or the running of area campaigns during the public phase of the program. Because area campaigns require major staff support and intense effort on the part of many volunteers, it is especially helpful to develop a time schedule for this part of the program. Kent

E. Dove, vice president for external affairs, Rice University, developed the following model calendar for an area campaign. The calendar will vary depending upon the area, the number of prospects to be solicited, and the size of gifts to be solicited.

First week:
1. Chair and staff representative meet to discuss the plans.
   a. From completed prospect evaluation, determine number of campaign workers needed to solicit prospects.
   b. Select division leaders.
   c. Set up the campaign calender, including dates of all organizational meetings, the solicitation committee meeting, kickoff reception, and the report and planning meetings.
   d. Determine and tentatively engage places for the solicitation committee meeting and the kickoff reception.
   e. Discuss arrangements for processing the necessary letters to be mailed over the chair's signature.
2. Chair begins enlistment of division leaders.

Second week:
1. Meeting of chair, division leaders, and staff representatives. Review the campaign program and begin enlistment of other volunteer workers.
2. Mail chair's invitation to the kickoff reception to all area alumni and other special guests.
3. Division leaders begin enlistment of team members.

Third week:
1. As campaign workers are enlisted, mail letter announcing date of solicitation committee meeting.
2. Release announcement of appointment of chair to appropriate news media.
3. Set campaign goal.

Fourth week:
1. Chair calls division leaders to check on progress of enlistment of team members.
2. Continue mailing letters announcing date of solicitation committee meeting.

Fifth week:
1. Campaign solicitation committee meeting (training and information session); workers are assigned prospects.
2. Workers call assigned prospects to remind of kickoff reception.

Sixth week:
1. *Kickoff reception.*
2. On day after kickoff reception, mail brochure and chair's letters to all area alumni who are not scheduled for personal solicitation.

3. Begin solicitation of campaigners on the day following the reception. Chair should solicit division leaders; division leaders solicit team members.

4. Begin solicitation of all prospects.

5. Following the kickoff reception, weekly progress reports will be mailed to all solicitors through a campaign newsletter prepared by the area chair and the staff representative.

Seventh week:

Hold first report meeting.

Eighth week:

Hold second report meeting.

Ninth week:

Hold third report meeting.

Tenth week:

Hold fourth report meeting.

Eleventh week:

1. If necessary, hold a fifth report meeting.
2. Make final check on outstanding pledge cards.
3. Chair sends letter of appreciation to all campaign workers.
4. Victory celebration with workers at final report meeting as goal is achieved!

Sometimes special circumstances make it possible for an institution to conduct a successful capital program without using the area campaign strategy. For example, when Sweet Briar College ran a five-year comprehensive development program with a goal of $12.1 million, we did not use area campaigns for the general solicitation of our constituencies. Our plan was to strengthen the annual giving program of the college to the point that all alumnae, parents, and friends thought of their annual gift as a campaign contribution. We listed the annual giving needs among the eight specific program goals of the campaign; the target was $5.2 million, 43 percent of the total capital program. All alumnae and parent organizations were strengthened by this intense effort, and annual support rose from $250,000 to over $1 million by the end of the program. Because of the strength of the existing annual giving organization, the college was able to establish a new $5,000 annual giving club and to initiate a sophisticated reunion class gifts program, both of which resulted in a significant increase in annual giving. At the same time, all donors to the Alumnae and Parents Funds were encouraged to support the college's capital campaign through their annual gift.

Using the annual giving organization in place of geographic area campaigns made it possible for a small group of volunteers to solicit the major gift prospects for capital pledges in addition to their annual gifts. Over 700 personal calls were made to prospects who had the potential of contributing $10,000 or more. We held only one cultivation activity for top prospects in our five largest geographic locations. Organizing kickoff events did not take much staff time, which meant staff were able to spend more time working with volunteers on the annual giving program and assisting the chair of the development committee, the president, and other top volunteers in the solicitation of major gifts.

Since we wanted to give every member of the constituency an opportunity to make a campaign pledge over a period of years, at the end of the campaign we tried a variation on the phone-mail program used several years ago at Yale University. We asked all nondonors and individuals who had contributed at a modest level to consider three-year pledges to the college. This phone-mail solicitation took place during the last six months of the five-year comprehensive development program.

The final results of the Sweet Briar campaign were $15.2 million in cash and pledges or 26 percent over the initial goal of $12.1 million. Annual alumnae participation averaged over 50 percent each year. The college continues to enjoy the benefits of a very strong annual giving program. In short, the Sweet Briar campaign illustrates how essential it is that the campaign calendar be realistic for each institution's particular circumstances and that it be adapted to its unique needs.

Some of the ideas presented in this chapter came from CASE's annual Capital Campaign Conference. *Capital Ideas* by M. Jane Williams provided the phase and year-by-year models. In my review of related literature, staff members at CASE and the National Society of Fund-Raising Executives provided valuable assistance. The literature made it clear that little specific documentation is available on the subject of the campaign calendar. This means that the advancement professional must use good judgment in analyzing the resources of the institution he or she represents. The campaign calendar has to reflect what can be done within a reasonable period of time, allowing for flexibility and for the modest changes in direction that may become necessary.

Don't we all wish we could simply "Begin at the beginning...and go on till we come to the end: then stop"?

Chapter 18

Campaign Mechanics

Scott G. Nichols
Dean for Development and
Director of Alumni/ae Affairs
Harvard Law School

Every campaign has that dreadful moment when we realize that good planning and committed major gift prospects are not enough. We must also tend to the logistical details that are endemic to campaigning. While well-planned campaigns are generally successful, few campaigners feel that they have successfully dealt with all the logistics. Individually, they may not seem important but collectively they can mean the difference between success or failure. The greatest value, however, of good campaign mechanics usually lies in the future. Considering the lengthy gestation of major gifts, we should be keenly aware that a well-run fully organized and documented capital campaign can pay direct, major dollar returns in the future.

This chapter covers two major areas that often receive insufficient attention and resources: documentation and organization.

Documentation

We've all heard about old so-and-so who ran a successful campaign "out of his head"—no paperwork. Most of us nod approvingly and agree that ours should be an endeavor of people, not paper. But the history of campaigning has shown us again and again the arrogance of conducting a poorly documented or unrecorded campaign. Files that are kept in someone's head are of little future value.

Nichols was formerly the associate vice president for development at DePaul University.

Moreover, "one-brain" files generally get much less accurate over time, are subject to only one interpretation, and are often difficult to locate. The best development officer mortgages his or her institution's future when the files are not in writing. But good paperwork begins well before the first prospect is seen.

The campaign plan/manual. Every campaign must have a written operating plan. It should start with the institutional background leading to a feasibility study. It should include the feasibility study summary, the case statement, the current state of fund raising at the institution, detailed objectives, complete organization plans (staff and volunteer), calendar, gift tables, named gift opportunities, job descriptions for leaders and workers, and campaign policies for accounting and recognition. Any items that indicate the who, what, where, when, why, and how must be covered. Many campaigners develop two plans. One is for internal use and includes prospect names; the other, for key volunteers, leaves out names.

Besides being an operational guide, a written plan also serves as a historical tool. It has particular value beyond the development office. You can circulate copies of the campaign manual marked "confidential" to key officers and top volunteers to show them the strong planning that has gone into the campaign. You will need to update and amend the manual at least quarterly to incorporate the midcourse corrections that invariably occur.

Every development staff member, especially key support staff personnel, should have a copy of the campaign manual. When you make up your distribution list, bear in mind that all the people who receive a copy of the campaign manual will see themselves as part of the inside team. Those who don't get a copy may feel excluded. The existence of the planning document is not enough. It should be comprehensive, current, and broadly circulated.

Solicitation manual. The ultimate moments in campaigns are those wherein people are asked to give. Therefore, you need a guide to the actual solicitation itself. A written "how-to" manual is often as useful to staff as it is to volunteers in outlining the background, purpose, and individual characteristics of the current effort. It should include simple but essential information about the institution, campaign goals, and anticipated responses with follow-up suggestions. You should distribute this document to *every* volunteer in the organization. For those people who believe they already know all there is to know about solicitation, you can stamp "for your information" on the cover.

Reports. I cannot overemphasize the importance of written reports. More volunteers are lost in a campaign, I believe, because of lack of information than for any other reason. Internal problems arise most frequently from lack of information about campaign goals, strategy, and progress. You can address both of these problems with written reports.

Campaign planning manuals should include a section on who will receive regular reports and how frequently. At minimum, you should be sending monthly and quarterly reports. Reporting is an area where *more* is more.

Use a newsletter bulletin on campaign letterhead for most of your internal audiences but distribute a more formal printed version to the general constituency. The dollar progress to date should be either part of the headline or the whole headline for the front-page story. Include in-depth profiles of donors and leadership workers. Always put in your goals, repackaging them in various forms to avoid repetition. Above all, stress the major objectives of the campaign and the need for gifts at the upper level.

Proposals and pledge statements. Even though we all agree that "people, not proposals, raise money," it is difficult for people to do so *without* proposals. Increasingly, major gift prospects are taking long periods of time to determine their level of support. You don't want prospective donors to have to rely on their memory of a conversation as they ponder. Like corporate and foundation prospects, individuals appreciate a well-reasoned written document that makes the request and justifies it.

Although each approach must be individualized for each prospect, certain components are common to all good proposals. A cover or title page that incorporates your campaign logo or theme is a good beginning. A succinct case statement—be leery of more than one page—is a must. Then you should focus on specific objectives that reflect the interests of the prospect. The heart of the proposal is a concise, straightforward request for a specific dollar figure for a specific campaign objective. I prefer a personalized letter from the president as the prefatory page. You might also want to include a section on ways you would like to recognize the particular prospect's gift.

How long should the proposal be? This is always a matter of debate. Suffice it to say that some effective proposals are long and some are short. Clarity and personalization are the essentials. Twenty pages of a strong, succinct case can be as compelling to one prospect as two pages are to another. Well before the first ask is made to the first prospect, you need to have in written form the core elements for all campaign proposals. Very often you will need to spend some money to this end by hiring a professional writer/consultant.

Pledge cards are synonymous with campaigning. Yet their use is not what people usually think it is. We've all received pledge cards in the mail. But pledge cards in the capital campaign are used for far more than just direct mail. They serve as a focal point in personal solicitation; they are the documentation of a gift; and, in some instances, they can be a legal commitment. Design your pledge cards so volunteers can use them easily. Pledge cards can help you ensure that a donor's gift meets his or her preferences and complies with campaign guidelines. Specifically, make sure the pledge card includes the following information:

- amount;
- form of gift (cash, securities, real estate, and so on);
- payment schedule (with starting date);
- restrictions;
- how the donor would like the gift credited (jointly with spouse, anonymously, in family name); and
- signature.

I like to put the following on the pledge card: "I/We understand that this pledge is made in good faith but is not legally binding should I or my family encounter unforeseen circumstances." This allays the fear many donors have that they may suddenly need the money for family obligations. A typed, one-page statement of intent can be used as effectively as a printed pledge card.

Acknowledgements. The written thank you is not only a prerequisite, it is an art form and cultivation tool. Given the import of campaign gifts, you need to have in place from the start a mechanism to thank donors quickly, accurately, and personally. For gifts and pledges at the $1,000-plus level, consider multiple, written thank yous. They should come from the top people and be on high-quality stationery with a personal signature. Customizing these letters to express personal appreciation should not be left to junior staff. Liberal use of copies shows the donor you want to tell important people about this important commitment. Keep copies of the letters as part of the donor's permanent record.

Minutes and memos. Contact with prospects and workers is the highest priority in documenting the campaign. You should report as frequently and in as much detail as possible decisions made either on strategy or in response to a solicitation. Keep minutes of all formal meetings of any campaign working group. Besides noting attendees, agenda, decisions that are made, and other obvious concerns, try to report on the attitudes and feelings of those involved. Note any dissension and explain decisions. Circulate the minutes within a few days of the meeting. Staff should be responsible for this paperwork to ensure its accuracy and appropriateness. When you plan your next campaign, knowing who favored what strategy or who knows what prospects can be an invaluable blueprint.

Note cultivation contacts in memo form. Make sure a memo goes in the file for each solicitation. Details recorded immediately can guide follow-up strategy later. If you don't like to ask your volunteers to write memos—and who does?—your staff can interview the solicitors and do the appropriate file recording. The larger the solicitation, the more detail you need. The solicitor's impressions as well as quotes from the prospect should be included. You can also use copies of these important file notes to inform others about progress (or lack thereof) with prospects. I am a particular fan of memos that end with a section on "Follow-up/next steps."

A growing number of institutions have started using contact reports. Staff and volunteers are asked to write quick notes on these forms whenever they have any contact with upper-level prospects. The reports can then be sent to a central repository (e.g., research, major gifts office) where they form an important record on the prospect.

The other paperwork. Besides those documents we've discussed, you will need the following items:
- prospect research reports;
- prospect screening forms;
- named gift opportunities;
- solicitation assignment sheets;
- kickoff plan;
- budget sheets and reports;
- solicitation results forms; and
- audio-visual resources.

Organization

No campaign has ever suffered from being too well organized. How complicated your organization need be depends on how many resources you have and how many staff members are available. Whether complex or simple, your organizational structure will require some paperwork.

Organizational charts. A diagram of the volunteer organization is a must. You will use it liberally when you recruit leaders and workers, and you will also want to include it in various publications. An organizational chart is not important just because it illustrates the extent or range of your workforce. Rather, its value lies in the fact that it shows that you have developed a well-structured, rational organization working toward a common goal, with clear, defined relationships between and among the various branches. Although frequently overlooked, a staff chart is equally important, and it should show the relationship and volunteer coverage of the professional staff.

Charts are great aids. I suggest you use lots of them, especially in strategic spots—conference rooms, lobbies, and reception areas of key institutional officers, for example. There are as many charts to make as there are aspects of a campaign to consider. You can use charts for training sessions, recruitment, or briefing meetings, and for display and motivation. I recommend that you prepare charts for the following:

- campaign goals by objectives;
- campaign goals by levels of giving;
- campaign goals by source (alumni, friends, corporations, foundations, and so on);
- campaign goals by college (or department, unit, and so on);
- fund-raising history (dollar results by year);
- donor history (number of donors by year);
- volunteer structure;
- giving trend analyses (corporate giving, foundation giving, matching gifts, estate giving, endowment growth, parent giving, trustee giving, unrestricted giving, and so on);
- alumni giving participation; and
- endowment comparisons (and endowment per student comparisons).

Prospect tracking. The need to track the upper few percent of our constituency has always been a fact of campaign life. Monitoring cultivation, solicitation, and other activities enables you to provide the necessary information to staff about progress. You need to review major gift prospect work on a *weekly* basis.

The advent of the personal computer (PC) gives every development operation the technological capability to track many prospects by category. Personal computers can easily handle detailed records or in-depth research reports on many hundreds if not thousands of upper-level prospects. A PC enables you to combine good research information on wealth and attitude with campaign variables such as dollar objective, potential solicitor, intended month of solicitation, and primary staff manager.

Because software for major gift tracking is currently very limited, many of the more sophisticated development offices have created their own software and willingly share their expertise. Development offices that still employ the 3 x 5 card are behind the times. And if you think a mainframe computer can track a relatively small percentage of the data base constituency quickly and easily, you probably haven't worked extensively with a large mainframe. We are in an era when the personal computer is an ideal tool.

The common categories used for tracking reflect customary gift levels: leadership, major, special, and general. As you probably organized your volunteer structure to solicit by these categories, it makes sense to organize the tracking systems in the same manner, except, of course, for the general gifts level where the prospect universe is too cumbersome for individual tracking.

At complex institutions, several units within the institution might approach the same prospect. To avoid duplicate solicitation, you need centralized prospect clearance. This is a major function of a prospect tracking system. It may not eliminate competition or friction between factions that want to approach the same prospect, but it certainly affixes accountability. Moreover, when you have the ability to generate current information sorted by a variety of variables, your staff and volunteer meetings should function much more smoothly.

Meetings. Volunteers are getting pickier. Increasing competition for volunteer time has made all of us more wary of going to meetings that waste our time. How many times have you sat in a one-hour meeting that should have been over in 15 minutes? We need to try to make the numerous meetings required by campaigning as efficient and effective as they can be. Here are some organizational tips:

1. Always use a written agenda for meetings of volunteers and for internal or staff meetings. This shows professionalism, good organization, and, as they say in the business world, your intention to "stick to the knitting." If possible, send the agenda to participants before the meeting.

2. Always stick to the time limits previously specified. Consider that you've made a contract with attendees to keep to announced starting and ending times. Starting late or extending the meeting is, at the very least, discourteous.

3. Take notes. Show that matters discussed are important enough to be accurately and immediately recorded.

4. Keep staff participation limited. Rarely should staff run a meeting in which volunteers participate. Staff can usually be most effective when they see themselves as aggressive listeners. Especially annoying is the know-it-all staff member who talks too much and listens too little.

5. Remember audience dynamics. Review room temperature, noise level, chair comfort, lighting, and room size (not too crowded, not too empty); be sure to provide a warm welcome, name tags, ashtrays and a nonsmoking section (if needed), and refreshments. If you always use the same meeting room, your staff will be able to fine-tune the dynamics.

6. Use visual aids extensively. Charts and slides have a much greater impact than pieces of paper. Whenever you see an option to reduce the number of papers at a meeting, use it.

7. Document. Minutes to any meeting can serve as the mandatory memo to the file. Follow-up or thank-you letters to attendees are always appropriate.

8. Prepare scripted presentations for top volunteers. At important meetings, key leaders should not only have outlines that summarize major points, they should have the precise wording. Though you should certainly consider the preferences of your volunteer leaders, I am a strong believer in fully scripting the presentation parts of any major gift solicitation. Top leaders generally expect to be given thorough preparation.

9. Keep the pace brisk. To ensure efficiency, keep meetings moving along at a good clip. People can absorb information more quickly than we can disseminate it verbally. Reserving time at the end of a meeting for questions or general discussion can keep matters substantive. Staff can bring the meeting back to the main point by responding to distracting or extraneous questions with the magic words, "Let me pursue that with you after the meeting."

Meetings necessary to a campaign include those for screening, prospecting, training, reporting progress, policy making, and assignment. You should plan all the meetings to make the most of participants' valuable time. Those meetings that introduce the campaign to strategic groups are particularly crucial. Many institutions use an all-day retreat for trustees to make the critical decisions to launch the campaign. This is perhaps the most important meeting in the entire course of a campaign. A retreat can also breathe new life into a campaign that is suffering the midlife doldrums. A single day or multi-day retreat for staff is superb for clarifying direction and raising morale.

During a campaign, every significant meeting in the normal course of running the institution should include an item on the campaign. Trustee and senior executive meetings and key committee meetings of faculty and staff should include campaign overviews and updates.

Gift and pledge tracking and acknowledgement. Before you receive your first pledge, you should have a system ready to track pledges and thank donors. Computer tracking is a must, be it on a PC or mainframe. Even if you must do tracking on 3 x 5 cards, these are the essentials to record:
- total amount pledged;
- gift type (outright, estate, combination, gift-in-kind);
- gift restrictions; and
- payment schedule.

The date on which a pledge reminder should be sent should trigger the payment schedule. It's useful to code for annual, semiannual, quarterly, or monthly reminders. With good terminal operators, a pledge tracking system can subsist with a simple flag to generate a list of those whose pledge payment is due month by month. But major and leadership pledges should be tracked and verified manually.

You don't need to send fancy reminders to donors, and you don't need to be indirect. Reminders are actually a sort of gracious bill. A crisp, businesslike reminder shows how important the gift is to the institution.

The reminder should be standardized in design, and the information on it, especially for larger donors, should be checked manually. Like an erroneous acknowledgement letter, an inaccurate pledge payment reminder can ruin years of good cultivation and successful solicitation. A reminder generally includes name, preferred mailing address, amount due at this time, total pledge, previous payments, gift restriction, matching qualification, and space for comment. Always include an envelope.

Reminders reflect the first rule of fund raising—in order to get, you must ask. Even when pledges are made in total good faith, donors need reminders. Payment rates and fulfillment percentages are a direct reflection of how well the staff reminds donors to send in their pledge installments. Exact statistics are hard to come by but it is commonly believed that, in most campaigns, 95 percent of the pledges will be fulfilled with a good reminder system. Dollars paid on pledges very often exceed the initial pledge; sometimes donors are conservative with their initial pledge and then increase their gifts over the life of the campaign. Collecting everything and more in a campaign is proof positive that your pledge tracking and reminder systems work.

Once you receive a gift or pledge payment, you need to acknowledge it. An acknowledgement serves as an expression of appreciation, a verification of the gift and its terms, and a tax receipt. When you are designing an acknowledgement system, remember that you can't thank people too quickly, too much, or too personally. Many offices try to send out the first acknowledgement within 48 hours of receipt of the gift. With a good gift and pledge tracking system, this is an attainable goal in the era of word processing.

Only the budget limits how many thank yous we can send to each donor. Most of us have found that a simple postcard acknowledgement is cost effective for the small donor, as are computer-generated acknowledgements. For midlevel donors, perhaps those in the $100 to $999 level, a first-class, personalized letter from a top volunteer or executive officer of the institution works well. At the $1,000 and up level, gift acknowledgement takes on a whole new meaning.

When I first started in the business of development, I was told by many veterans that a good development officer spends 10 percent of his or her time on gift acknowledgements, almost all of which is devoted to current or future major gift prospects. Whether it is called gift acknowledgement or stewardship, thanking donors should be a daily, high-priority item. I believe that any donor of $1,000 or more should receive a written thank you from the chief executive and the top volunteer leader in the organization. Don't be shy about including others and don't hesitate to send copies freely. We need to spread the good news about a gift.

Don't overlook the telephone in gift acknowledgement. Several institutions have enlisted faculty to pick up the phone and call all donors above a certain level.

Personalizing thank yous is an art form of the highest order. Formula letters deceive no one. Time spent and depth of the sentiment expressed are readily apparent in this era of impersonalization. The best staff work we can perform in this area is to convince the chief executive and top volunteer to acknowledge significant gifts personally. One suggestion—keep the letters brief. You don't have to be wordy to thank someone. In fact, a few sentences are usually enough to express the institution's sincere appreciation.

If we tend to spend too little time thanking donors, we often spend too much time on gift recognition items. Trinkets and beads, from lapel pins to oil portraits, siphon off valuable time, money, and energy. Major donors, the core of any campaign constituency, are not motivated by the size of the plaque they are promised or the football tickets they will receive. So keep gift recognition items to a minimum; use them after a gift has been negotiated; and make sure they are a surprise. A recognition item has its greatest impact when it comes as a reaction to the gift. The same can be said for recognition events. They should be a part of the never-ending process of cultivation. When they are designed to say thank you to large groups, they should be infrequent but first-rate affairs. Donors do not want to see the institution eat up their support, either figuratively or literally. But they do expect that money spent on recognizing substantial gifts will be spent well. And that, of course, means spending first-class money in a first-class way to encourage first-class philanthropy.

Finally, recognition should include the public acknowledgement of gift and giver. Publicize names of donors (always with their consent) in press releases (when the gift is large enough) and in newsletters, publications, and so forth. An honor roll or listing of donors to the campaign is mandatory. Most institutions do this on an annual basis.

Challenges. One of the best techniques for upgrading giving within or without a campaign is challenge giving. A donor or group of donors makes a commitment contingent on others making or increasing their commitments.

Challenges work well. They are especially effective when a major giver agrees to match increased giving, up to a certain maximum, of a broad-based group (alumni, parents, or friends). Some challenges are linked to achieving a particular number of donors, always a substantial increase over the previous year. The extra dimension of a challenge spurs people into action. In a complex campaign, the challenge can be a way of linking the small and the large donor in a common goal with deadlines that must be met. A challenge can breathe new life into a sagging campaign. It can focus on a particular area of a campaign, such as the library, athletics, scholarships, or gift clubs.

Budgeting. How much should a campaign cost and how should it be paid for? Unfortunately for educational institutions, public attention on fund-raising costs has been either negative or focused on unrealistically low figures. For organizations like the Salvation Army, keeping costs to a minimum is crucial to their ability to attract public support. They are quick to point out that their fund-raising costs are only a very few percent of total dollars raised. At the other extreme are organizations that spend exorbitant amounts of money to raise their dollars.

The range for most educational fund-raising campaigns appears to be from 5 to 15 percent. The larger the campaign, the more likely it is that costs will be at the lower end. Campaigns relying on broad-based support tend to have costs at the upper end of the range.

You need to ponder many historical factors before you determine which end of the scale is most appropriate for your institution. The preceding campaign should always be a key factor. A successful prior campaign in the not-too-distant past (less than 10 years) can mean that building a campaign organization or educating your constituency to a campaign will not be very costly. Campaigns with little historical momentum must look at higher costs.

There are four common models used in financing a campaign—line item budgeting, unrestricted gift allocation, gift tax, and gift income generation.

Most campaigns are funded by line item budgeting—that is, the costs of the campaign are absorbed as a line item within the overall budget of the institution. This puts extra strain on a usually tight operating budget.

If the campaign is financed through unrestricted gift allocation, the bills are paid by all or a portion of the unrestricted campaign contributions. This method works only when unrestricted goals are incorporated into the campaign in the initial stages. A campaign using this model must place heavy emphasis on increasing unrestricted giving in order to raise enough money to cover costs.

The third method is the gift tax. In essence, every campaign objective is taxed a few percent to provide for fund-raising costs. Each dollar objective incorporates fund-raising costs. If you use this method, you must plan for it in the earliest stages. You cannot add to your dollar goals once you have announced them.

Finally, the method I prefer is gift income generation. At DePaul, we put campaign payments in income-generating accounts for a year or more, and we used the interest income for budget relief. While this has a terrific advantage in that it does not strain the operating budget, it does present a cash flow problem. Not all gifts are available for investment, and cash flow irregularities can play havoc even with well-planned budgets.

Campaign financing can be a disaster if you do not address the problem squarely and early. Recognizing that increased gift income requires an increased budget is the first step.

Policy matters. No two campaigns are alike. Indeed, they reflect the rich diversity inherent in American education. But everyone planning a capital campaign must resolve, with the aid of key volunteers, the following questions, preferably by written policy statements:

1. When shall we start accepting pledges? When shall we finish? What is the last date for payment on pledges?

2. Will we accept estate commitments? If so, on what terms and how old must the donor be?

3. Will gifts-in-kind be accepted and on what terms? How about real estate and art? Who will do the appraisal?

4. Who will decide campaign crediting for gifts not clearly within the campaign parameters?

5. Will we count gifts from nonprivate sources?

6. What are minimum endowment levels for chairs? scholarships?

7. Will individuals receive credit for a matching corporate gift?

As you can see, campaign mechanics concern far more than just the petty details of the capital effort. Without attention to logistics, the campaign won't function and the dollars won't come in. And that, after all, is what it's all about.

Chapter 19

Solicitation Methods and Training

Sara L. Patton
Vice President for Development
The College of Wooster

In most successful capital campaigns, volunteers are involved at every level of the enterprise, and their efforts prove critical to the outcome of the campaign. Once you have identified and recruited your volunteers, you must make sure that they understand the campaign's goals, organization, and strategic plan, including the vital role that they themselves will play—as individuals and as a group—in making the campaign succeed.

The degree to which volunteers internalize the campaign's objectives and act to achieve them depends in large part on the effectiveness of the training programs you provide. You cannot expect volunteers to embrace a plan that they do not understand or that they cannot readily see themselves putting into action. Clearly, the training program deserves the involvement and commitment of the campaign's leadership as well as every member of its staff. Volunteers will take their assignments more seriously if you demonstrate that they are worthy of your best efforts and your wholehearted support. That means attention from the top, including the president, trustees, campaign chair, and key committee chairs. Volunteers function best when they can see that what they do will make a difference, and that how well they do it will be noticed and appreciated by persons they respect. No matter how glorious the "cause," few individuals will serve it unceasingly without some attention and feedback from a human being, and preferably from several of them.

When your volunteer training programs are planned and executed with imagination, intelligence, and good humor, they become superb cultivation opportunities. Of course, not every prospective donor will be a campaign volunteer, but every volunteer should certainly be a donor. The training process is, in fact, a rehearsal for the real work of the campaign.

As professional fund raisers, our task is to make it as easy as possible for prospective donors to say "yes." Similarly, we must give our volunteers the tools they need to do what we ask of them. Donors must understand why their personal participation matters before we can expect them to make a "stretching" capital gift commitment. Volunteers, to be effective, must understand why their individual assignments contribute to the end result in an essential and compelling way.

How, then, can we structure our orientation and training sessions for maximum effectiveness? Training volunteers in groups according to their campaign responsibilities works well. Volunteer leaders, who will be recruiting and perhaps even training other volunteers, need special attention and support so that they feel like insiders and will be enthusiastic and knowledgeable advocates of the campaign in their own spheres of influence.

Bringing volunteers together as a group fosters enthusiasm, a sense of excitement, and a winning attitude. If key volunteers are aware from the outset of what their part of the campaign seeks to do, and how that part relates to the other parts of the effort, they will be more likely to follow through with their assignments.

For example, to launch the volunteer action phase of Wooster's campaign, we invited the 65 volunteer chairs of our regional committees to come to the campus for a weekend orientation and training session. We offered to pay expenses for participants and stressed the importance of the meeting. We also invited members of the national steering committee, including the campaign's national chair, the chair of the board of trustees, and other top-level leaders.

The event took a great deal of planning, and it was worth every minute. Some 60 of our 65 chairs came to the campus from across the country. They assembled on Friday evening for a social hour hosted by a local trustee and followed by a festive dinner. We introduced each volunteer so that participants got some sense of the talent enlisted for the campaign.

Saturday morning was devoted to training sessions. Wooster's president, board chair, and national campaign chair made brief remarks to the group and then answered questions about the college and the campaign. We made sure that they emphasized the role of volunteers as a key strategy in the campaign.

Then we divided the group into smaller units for two fund-raising practice sessions, with members of the development staff as leaders and participants. Our session on deferred giving methods and options for donors was an hour-long "short course" taught by the college's deferred giving officer and a trustee who is an attorney in the field. We hoped this training would remind volunteers that there are more ways of giving than writing a check on the spot. We also wanted to demonstrate that the college had knowledgeable staff who were ready to assist donors identified as deferred giving prospects.

The second session was called "Making the First Call." Staff and volunteers did improvisations of conversations between volunteers and prospective donors. This brought the script to life and gave volunteers some practice in making the rhetoric of the campaign their own. They also enjoyed the "living theater" aspect.

The improvisations allowed participants to express their anxieties as well as their enthusiasm. For instance, at one point the staff member playing the role of the volunteer asked the audience to ask her the one question they were most afraid of getting when they made their own calls. The exercise often became hilarious, but many volunteers later said that they felt more confident after having heard the hard questions fielded effectively.

The goal of the weekend was to send volunteer leaders back to their regional committees with facts and figures about the college; a sound knowledge of the campaign's goals, organization, and management; and a heightened commitment to their task.

They also took home a training packet of materials summarizing the content of the weekend session. This packet included standard capital campaign training materials such as the following items:

- campaign brochure, including the campaign case statement;
- operating plan for volunteers (a definition of their role);
- "Gift Opportunities" paper;
- communications plan;
- "Contributions...How To Make Them" (deferred giving options);
- one pledge card and return envelope;
- Fact Sheet (the institution today);
- "Procedure for Solicitations" paper (sequence of calls, content, reports);
- prospect report form (to be completed by volunteers);
- summary of objectives for volunteer contacts;
- script for personal calls;
- "What Do I Say If...." (possible answers to impossible questions);
- timetable for volunteers;
- staff responsibilities to volunteer committees; and
- letter to prospective volunteers (for volunteer leaders to recruit other volunteers).

Whatever the volunteer's particular assignment or level of responsibility, he or she is likely to want answers to three basic questions:

- What are you asking me to do?
- How am I supposed to go about it?
- Will I be able to do the job successfully?

To answer the first question, you need job descriptions for volunteers that state the number of calls they will be expected to make, how much time they will have to make them, and the anticipated outcome of the calls. Volunteers ask this question because they are concerned about commitment: Just how large an investment of their time and energy is required?

It is important to present the facts honestly to volunteers without scaring them away. If your plan allows them to schedule their time with some degree of flexibility, while still meeting the demands of the campaign timetable, the assignment will seem more manageable.

For example, in Wooster's campaign we included the paragraph below in a letter that volunteer chairs used for recruitment. It helped to enlist over 1,500 alumni volunteers who served throughout the country, making personal calls and visits to other alumni and friends of the college. We emphasized the positive, stressing both the importance of the task and the support that would be available to volunteers from the professional staff.

> The time commitment required is small when compared to the enormous potential benefit to the College. You will receive excellent training from Wooster's professional staff and complete information about any assignments you might be given. You will be asked to work with no more than 15 prospects, total, between now and December 1984, and campaign strategy allows you to make your calls whenever it is most convenient for you. In the fall of 1982 there will be an introductory session for all volunteers and perhaps two or three meetings thereafter throughout the year. The majority of actual requests will be made in 1983-84 after we have all become familiar with the structure, goals, and strategies of the campaign.

To answer the other two questions ("How am I supposed to go about it?" and "Will I be able to do the job successfully?") we presented our campaign strategies and techniques we planned to implement them. I believe that the most effective way of inspiring confidence is to get volunteers to use the script and to practice it as described above. Scripts are a key resource for volunteers. Although they will probably adapt the script to their own vernaculars, the basic message of the campaign will be presented clearly and consistently by all volunteers.

You want your training session to make volunteers feel at ease using the script and other materials available to them. Volunteers who know what information is needed, what support is available, and also what to say (and how to say it) will have the confidence to give the job their best try.

Types of solicitations

Most capital campaigns, by the time they are completed, will use each of the three basic solicitation methods: personal presentations, telephone, and direct mail. Each method has advantages and drawbacks. Timing, cost, and personnel required (both staff and volunteers) will influence your decision as to which to use.

Common sense dictates that personal attention should intensify and increase as the stakes get larger. Therefore, it is not surprising that personal contacts are more important in capital campaign strategies than in annual fund programs.

Personal presentations are *essential* for major gift prospects and can also be effective with donors below the major level. The personal call has the greatest impact upon the donor, who must consider the appeal and participate in discussion with the person who asks for the gift. This face-to-face exchange has an immediacy and a psychological weight rarely found in boilerplate proposals or mailings. Because the prospect is actively involved in the exchange, the caller gains new information that enables the proposal to be modified or enhanced if necesary.

A personal visit is an important research opportunity. It is the best way to gain a sense of the prospect's lifestyle, values, and priorities. For that reason alone, you should use this strategy for as many of the campaign's constituents as possible. In the Campaign for Wooster, for example, we set out to make a personal visit to *all* Wooster alumni in the United States. As one awestruck volunteer remarked: "That's 20,000 living rooms!" And it was, just about, though we did not get inside every one. The effort required over 1,500 volunteers from coast to coast. The college benefited not only in dollars raised, but in new information about a substantial number of alumni and friends.

A personal call underscores the message that the campaign's success really depends upon the efforts of key prospects and volunteers.

Telephone calls have less impact than a personal call but more than direct mail. You can use the telephone to follow up on personal visits or letters, to reinforce particular points of discussion, or to wrap up a pending proposal. A phone call is a great way to send a reminder, congratulate a victory, and convey any information quickly and directly.

Should you use the telephone extensively in capital campaigns? Certainly the phone call has gained wide acceptance for annual fund efforts. Most institutions have had phonathons of one kind or another so that their constituents are acquainted with the concept. But if your annual fund relies upon a telephone campaign each year, a similar effort for the capital campaign might be confusing to prospects. On the other hand, if you include the annual fund program in the capital fund goal, and if you use a double ask (that is, you ask the prospect to make an annual fund gift *every* year and a capital gift *once* during the course of the campaign), then using the phone to solicit annual fund gifts is probably quite effective. For one thing, it gives your volunteers another chance to talk about the campaign to prospective donors by casting the annual fund appeal in the context of the larger effort.

If the annual fund is *not* a factor in your capital campaign, you might use the phone to solicit campaign gifts below major or leadership levels. As any veteran of phonathons will know, telephoning on a broad scale can be expensive, time-consuming for staff and computer resources, and logistically complicated. But it can also be the most effective substitute for a personal visit.

Direct mail is best at conveying specific information at one time to members of a wide audience. Most capital campaigns use direct mail at key points to be sure that the constituency as a whole is aware of the progress of the drive. For example, you could send the campaign case statement, or brochure, to *all* prospects at the start of the campaign. In this way, everyone who will eventually be asked to participate will feel that they have been involved from the beginning. If you have challenge opportunities from individuals or foundations, you'd want to send out a direct mail announcement to get all the facts before the largest number of prospective donors in the shortest possible time. Direct mail is also good for campaign reports, updates, and major announcements. You probably have some prospects whom your volunteers cannot visit (alumni living abroad, for instance) and who must be asked to give by mail.

You can use your campaign's direct mail program to prepare and support personal contacts being made by volunteers and staff in the field. Direct mail can expose the leadership of the campaign to a wider audience. Not every prospect can be called on by the national chair, but the chair can write a letter that goes to many or all prospects.

You will need to review your direct mail strategies, like other elements of the campaign, as the campaign progresses. Timing is particularly important; don't miss an opportunity to share good news or a dramatic turn in the campaign.

Should you enclose a pledge card with a particular direct mail piece? This depends on the writer of the piece, the timetable for personal solicitations, and what other mailings are going out. Direct mail is likely to be the primary form of annual fund solicitations at most institutions, and those mailings should be coordinated so they don't "clash" with any campaign requests.

You can use the different solicitation methods together in most campaign cultivations. The summary of a "Suggested Procedure for Solicitation of Leadership Gifts" below was used in a successful campaign. Volunteers followed these guidelines when they called on prospects targeted to make capital gifts of $5,000 to $99,000. Members of the staff went over the guidelines in every volunteer training session we held.

Suggested Procedure for Solicitation of Leadership Gifts

Initial approach: Telephone for appointment or make appointment in person. Be direct, enthusiastic, and brief. You may see prospect at his or her home, in the office, or on neutral ground—whatever seems most comfortable.

First contact: Your goals for this first visit:

1. To establish rapport with individual. What are his or her interests generally? How close (or distant) does he or she feel to the College? What are family ties/commitments?

2. To create an awareness about the campaign—nationally and in the individual's own geographic area. Use campaign brochure, especially the needs summary page, and report success to date.

3. To find out what potential donor's interests at Wooster might be: "What do you think Wooster does well?" "What don't you like?"

Material to be left behind: Campaign brochure [a second copy—first had been sent previously by direct mail].

Second Contact: May be done by mail or by personal delivery.

1. Send written follow-up letter or information about any particular program interest, e.g., landscaping, computers, library, music.

2. Begin to mention what money can buy in terms of what you think donor's *potential* (*not* what you think he or she will give) is. (Use "Gift Opportunities" paper for ideas.) If you need additional information from college, get in touch with region head immediately.

Immediate follow-up to second contact: Telephone or see person to answer questions or provide additional information.

Third contact: This should be a personal visit.

    1. Ask individual for a gift to the campaign. Suggest how gift of $_____ could support area of donor's special interest.

    2. Discuss how gift can be made in order to accomplish donor's program objective.

    3. Give pledge card and fill it out at this visit, or ask donor to send it back to the College directly.

Fourth contact: Telephone call or note of appreciation for consideration, stressing important points of presentation.

Additional contacts: As necessary until decision is made and gift or pledge to the campaign is secured.

Final contact: Personal note of thanks from volunteer.

Note: It is important that region chairs are kept informed of all contacts so that they can make their reports to College staff support person (use contact report form).

Prospect matching

After you have decided on your solicitation methods, assembled your materials, and recruited and trained volunteers, you must now determine how to match volunteers with prospects. The person you select to make the ask can substantially affect the result. Obviously, no staff member or volunteer can know everyone personally, but there are ways of cultivating some common ground between volunteers and potential donors. How you organize the constituency depends upon the campaign's particular objectives and special projects. I've outlined some organization strategies below. You can use a combination of these elements to make assignments. As a rule, the more elements the solicitor and prospect have in common, the better the chance for success.

    1. *Class year.* At most colleges and universities, students—and therefore alumni—know more members of their own class than members of other classes. This strategy is used in many class agent annual fund programs.

    2. *Interest group.* Alumni also know people who shared an academic major or some extracurricular activity. For instance, you might approach physical education majors as a group for funds to build a field house; you might appeal to drama majors when you are raising money for a new theater.

    3. *Geography.* This could be a compelling consideration for prospects below major gift level. It's easier for volunteers to make personal calls in their own areas.

    4. *Affiliation with the institution.* Trustees, alumni, and parents have close ties to the institution. In most cases, a *like* affiliation makes for a more effective call—trustees call on trustees, alumni on alumni, and so on.

    5. *Past association/friendship.* Who knows whom? This consideration must

nearly always be secondary to other matching strategies. Nevertheless, many volunteers feel more comfortable calling on someone they know.

6. *Current career interests.* Doctors talk to doctors, lawyers to lawyers, teachers to teachers, and so on.

7. *Gift rating.* Insofar as possible, this strategy matches a volunteer of a certain giving potential with a prospect in the same category. It is especially effective when the volunteer has already made a gift at the targeted level. A prospect's rating or potential to give should not be confused with performance. In this instance, potential is more important.

All of these considerations apply to prospect-volunteer matches regardless of the prospect's rating. However, you should certainly try harder for a close match in the major and leadership gift categories simply because there is more at stake.

Often major gift committees will assign two or more people to cultivate a prospect and more than one person—the president and the campaign chair, for example—to make the formal request. When you make these decisions, the rules of common sense and courtesy should carry the day. Some people may feel threatened by a two-on-one approach; others will be flattered by top-level attention. If you have done prospect research and cultivation effectively, you should be able to trust your judgment of particular situations.

In summary, the right solicitor is one who fully understands the organization and strategy of the campaign. He or she is able to communicate the importance of the campaign with enthusiasm and confidence in a way that makes it appealing to the prospect and easy for him or her to participate in the effort.

Good training is worth the time it takes. Not only does it make the volunteers better at their jobs, but it provides cultivation for those who, by giving of themselves, make an invaluable commitment to our institutions.

Chapter 20

Public Relations Support for the Capital Campaign

Donald R. Perkins
Director, Public Information
Wittenberg University

C ontributions to higher education from all sources exceeded $6 billion in 1984-85. Estimates are that nearly $2 billion of that amount came from capital campaigns. In the future, an increasing number of the nation's colleges and universities will engage in capital campaigns. Further, most higher education institutions, while not in publicly announced capital campaigns, will nevertheless conduct repeated campaigns to secure funds for programs.

This constant challenge to solicit dollars from all sources makes public relations support a high priority. Public relations support for the capital campaign helps create, or enhance, a climate for giving in which the institution can raise funds of the amount and kind desired.

While public relations can make a significant contribution to the capital campaign, we must recognize that a campaign does not take place in a vacuum. We can't block out the period of time during which a capital campaign is to be conducted and declare that the institution will, for that span, foster good public relations. Good public relations must precede the campaign, go on during the campaign, and continue after the campaign goal has been reached. And that means good internal as well as external public relations.

If you are responsible for the public relations for your institution's capital campaign, you will need to make sure that faculty, staff, and students are informed about the campaign prior to its beginning and receive updates on its progress. The president's time is well spent at faculty, staff, and student meetings, where he or she explains campaign goals and how they will enhance teaching, learning, research, and the image of the institution.

Meetings with internal constituencies also provide opportunities to explain why the president and key administrators will frequently be away from campus. Time spent with your internal audiences pays dividends when you ask them to make campaign contributions and they give amounts that demonstrate to external constituencies that those who know the institution best are among its best supporters.

The more your internal constituents understand about the campaign, the more confidence they will have in it. It is important to explain that a percentage of the funds raised will be spent on special events that will help ensure that campaign goals are reached. This can help significantly to allay complaints about the costs of cultivation activities for donors. As your institution embarks upon a capital campaign, you want to create a communal spirit among your internal constituencies; you want them to feel, "We're all in this together."

Perhaps the most significant first step in good capital campaign public relations is to prove that the institution has defined and justified its need to raise funds. For this reason, you must establish your case long before the first donor is approached for a contribution. If an institution is seeking dollars for new buildings, it might be a good idea to hire consultants who study college learning environments. They can determine the total campus facility needs and document how more buildings will enhance teaching, learning, and research at the institution.

If your institution has never—or at least not in recent years—defined or redefined its mission and priorities, this would be a good time to do so in order to validate the institution's significance and its worthiness for support.

If your institution does not have a vital alumni program, before the capital campaign begins you will need to build renewed confidence in the institution among this most important constituency.

Donors need to know that their contributions are aiding an institution that is well managed and that sees its future clearly. You will need to convince some donors that the institution you are asking them to help is as well run as their successful businesses.

The public relations strategy for the campaign does not take place in a vacuum but must relate to the life of the institution, its history, and its ethos. Public relations plans should contribute to public understanding of how the institution reached its current stature, what it is doing to maintain and enhance its position, and what plans it has for its future.

Honesty is essential. Resist pressure, regardless of the source, to inflate the institution's image for the purpose of the capital campaign.

Because a campaign often works on many fronts, you need to know the target audiences for each phase of the campaign and the timing of solicitations. This enables you to construct a master public relations plan that works in tandem with fundraising efforts.

The most effective plan evolves from consultations with a broad range of people who will plan and conduct the fund raising. Their consensus on your plan will give it the validity it needs.

Your master plan should contain at least six elements:
- statement of mission;
- statement of priorities;

- target audiences;
- themes;
- methods; and
- evaluation.

Statement of mission

The statement of mission defines the purpose of public relations in the campaign, as in the following: "To increase awareness, understanding, and appreciation of the university among selected audiences in selected geographic areas with the aim of motivating support for the capital campaign."

Statement of priorities

The statement of priorities reflects the timetable for solicitations. A statement of priorities might note, for example: "A market-by-market approach will be made on a geographic basis. Each market will be addressed separately according to a timetable that corresponds to fund-raising efforts. The current timetable calls for beginning in the area of the college and expanding to regional and national geographic areas."

While the mission of public relations in a capital campaign remains constant, the priorities may change as the fund raisers alter strategy to keep gift levels high. You need to be aware of this possibility and, by keeping close contact with the fund raisers, change the direction and emphases of programs to reflect new strategy.

Target audiences

The fund raisers will determine the target audiences in the campaign. A combination of gift levels and geographic areas is a common mix. In this approach, campaign planners select a section of the country and establish gift levels for individuals, corporations, foundations, and all other gift sources. Another strategy is to focus on soliciting only individuals in a selected area, with corporations, foundations, and other prospects folded into a separate drive.

Target audiences include alumni, members of church constituencies, parents of past and current students, corporations, foundations, and old and new friends of the institution.

When plans call for soliciting individuals, the target audience might be further defined by income, such as "persons of affluence and influence with annual incomes of $100,000 or above."

Themes

The themes of the campaign catalog the primary strengths of the institution, those that make the greatest contribution to its stature. These themes should be repeated in all public relations materials. They help define or reinforce the institution in the minds of donors.

To develop themes appropriate to your institution, you would usually begin by noting the kind of institution it is—two year, four year, public, undergraduate, graduate, liberal arts, technical, medical, or law. Then, in separate short statements, you would describe additional outstanding qualities of the education offered, such as academic program, faculty, personal attention to students, type and academic rankings of students, successful alumni, and sound financial management.

The themes you use should emphasize aspects of the institution most likely to help motivate contributions. For example, themes that deal with teaching and learning—activities fundamental to any institution, regardless of size or character—often exert the greatest impact on donors. For this reason, you need to make sure that prospective donors are fully aware of the caliber of faculty and students. One way to translate this idea into campaign public relations is as follows: "Our professors are master teachers who care about their students and give them close personal attention. Our students are bright, imaginative people, who are a challenge to their professors."

Closely following teaching and learning in importance is the product—the graduate: "Our graduates are successful and credit the education they received at our institution with a major role in their career achievements."

Methods

Once you've developed the themes, or messages, you have to devise methods to deliver them to the target audience to motivate contributions. This task will probably occupy the major part of your time during a capital campaign.

First you'll need to know the timetable for campaign solicitation. Then you can coordinate activities that heighten visibility with active solicitation. You should implement these strategies at least one month ahead of the solicitations and continue them through the solicitation phase.

The degree of name recognition and acceptance your institution enjoys will vary in different solicitation areas. A capital campaign affords excellent opportunities to warm up institutional relations in some areas and to make new friends among media and other information gatekeepers in other areas.

A number of strategies can increase institutional visibility before and during the solicitation phase. You can also use them to introduce your campaign themes. These strategies include:
- on-site validators;
- faculty speakers on current topics;
- interviews with your president;
- targeted hometown stories and op-ed programs;
- special recognition for noted area residents; and
- leads to media on newsworthy alumni in their area.

On-site validators are media or media-related persons who reside in or near the areas to be impacted and who have a tie to the institution. They may be alumni or "alumni-like" persons, friends of the institution, present or past parents of students, or board members. Their role is to vouch for the credibility of the institution, the campaign, and its public relations effort. Using on-site validators is a good way to capture media attention.

Look in your institution's alumni guide, which usually lists graduates geographically, to locate alumni in the relevant areas. If you can't find enough media or media-related people, try to recruit persons of stature in the area who may not possess media skills but can serve as "door-openers" for your institution's public relations efforts. For example, one university got expert help in a key fund-raising area from the public relations director of a company whose president served on the institution's board of directors.

On-site validators can also serve in an advisory role. If you recruit them for a communications advisory committee, they can work closely with you to help you secure media attention for story ideas and campaign information. They can visit or make telephone calls or send notes to local media about ideas for stories; they can inquire about ideas or materials most likely to pique media interest. They can be especially helpful when it is time to prepare their areas for active solicitation.

This strategy works most effectively if you visit each member of the communications advisory committee in his or her area. You can also use this occasion to meet, with the member's aid, local media people.

If time and funds permit, you can invite the communications advisory committee to campus before the campaign begins and ask them to critique the master public relations plan, campaign publications, slide shows, and other fund-raising support materials.

It is especially helpful if at least one member of the communications advisory committee has expertise in radio and television, for these media are indispensable in campaign public relations.

Your institution's alumni office can also help you reach the media. The office can plan alumni meetings in solicitation areas and schedule a faculty member to speak on the hot topic of the day. Then, with the aid of the appropriate member of the communications advisory committee, you can alert the media in the area that an expert on a current topic will be in their vicinity. Offer to make the speaker available for interviews. This is best accomplished by a comprehensive letter clearly outlining the professor's expertise, followed by a telephone call to check level of interest. First, make sure the professor is willing to visit the media at their work sites and, if necessary, to arrive in the area early to allow time for interviews. This is the point where the "we're all in this together" spirit pays off.

The president of your institution is probably an expert on one or more topics in higher education and would be a prime candidate for interviews. Check the president's travel schedule to see if he or she will be visiting any of the fund-raising areas. Then follow up by making media appointments.

You can also use the time-honored hometown story to increase visibility in selected areas. Use the computer to identify students from the solicitation area. Determine which ones are engaged in truly newsworthy activities, not just routine membership in choirs, sororities, or fraternities. Look for possible feature stories about new or unusual class projects, study abroad, internships, or athletic achievements. Weekly newspapers are sometimes the best targets for these stories.

Similarly, an op-ed program of faculty opinions can be aimed at newspapers in fund-raising areas, thereby emphasizing the institution's learned faculty.

Research will likely identify an outstanding alumnus, board member, benefactor, or friend worthy of recognition in each fund-raising area. You can use recognition activities for this person to increase your institution's visibility and, if the timing is right, to launch an area campaign. For example, you might plan a dinner in his or her honor, and invite business, civic, education, and government leaders in the area. Give the media hard news and feature stories about the honoree before the event, provide interview opportunities, and invite members of the media to cover the dinner.

Perhaps one of your alumni, who lives in the campaign solicitation area, is engaged in a newsworthy career, hobby, or volunteer activity. A tip to appropriate media can result in stories mentioning your institution. Check the alumni news sections of alumni publications for possibilities.

Hard news stories about volunteers in the campaign should go to all media outlets serving areas where they reside. Be sure appropriate employee publications and house organs also receive this information.

During the campaign, look for news about the institution that originates locally but may be marketable to a wider audience. If you think a print story might have wider appeal, encourage the originating newspaper to make it available to the wire services, or send them a tear sheet with a note urging distribution. If a television station tapes a story on your campus and you think it might be newsworthy beyond the station's area, ask the station to send it to the regional centers operated by the networks for offering by satellite to affiliate stations throughout the region or the country. Although you can't target the information when this happens, it's too valuable an opportunity to miss. When appropriate, urge the TV station to take advantage of this system.

Capital campaigns often rely heavily on gifts from donors who reside in the institution's home state. You will need to maximize your use of newspapers, radio, and television to support solicitation of this important audience. For example, you might consider use of state wire services, a statewide feature service aimed at daily and weekly newspapers, and TV targeting of the state. A story taped on campus that may have statewide, but not regional or national, appeal can be dubbed on blank tapes by the originating station at low cost and sent to stations across the state. Most originating stations, if given credit for the story, are pleased to cooperate. Contact the stations before the dubbing to determine interest.

Holidays offer numerous possibilities for increasing name recognition across a state. The institution's choir can tape Christmas carols for use by TV stations. You can tape season's greetings of station-break length (less than 10 seconds) for television and then strip off the audio for radio stations. The station that agrees to do the taping should get exclusive use of the package in its viewing area. Blank videotapes are not expensive and dubbing costs are minor.

Your campaign public relations tasks begin well before the kickoff. You should be a member of the campaign's top strategy group, attend all campaign meetings and activities, and be privy to all exchanges of information about the campaign. Only by being a full partner can you make a maximum contribution. You will also need adequate staff and budgets commensurate with expectations.

You will need to establish special channels of communication with the national campaign chair and the president of the institution. During the campaign you must have ready access to both persons.

Planning public relations activities that will attend the campaign kickoff requires special care because, in the minds of media and other important persons, the kickoff sets the tone for the campaign.

At least one month before the campaign begins, you, in collaboration with a member of the communications advisory committee, should arrange meetings for the institution's president with editorial boards of leading newspapers within a 75- to 100-mile radius of the campus. The purpose of the visits is to acquaint top management of the press with the campaign, solicit editorial support and attention to campaign news, and issue an invitation to the news conference announcing the start of the campaign.

When appropriate, you should also arrange meetings for the same purpose with general managers and news directors of leading television and radio stations and with editors of regional and area magazines.

To ensure good attendance at the news conference announcing the campaign, send the media letters of invitation, over the president's signature. The letter need only say that news of major importance will be announced. Include a stamped return postcard so the media representatives can *RSVP*. If you don't get responses from key media, follow up with telephone calls.

Plan the news conference carefully and provide participants with prepared scripts. Make sure the campaign chair and the president are the central figures. You will need to schedule a rehearsal for all participants, preferably in the setting where the news conference will take place.

If the campaign is for new buildings or renovations, provide models or drawings. You also need to prepare a media information kit containing:

- a comprehensive news release about the campaign;
- copies of scripts used by news conference participants;
- biographies and photos of campaign leaders and the president;
- photos illustrating campaign goals; and
- copies of key campaign publications.

Videotape and record the news conference to provide a source of information for television and radio stations that did not send anyone. The taping and the recording will also provide the start of important campaign record-keeping.

A good nose for news is the best asset for capitalizing on campaign events after the kickoff. Look for opportunities deriving from the following:

- receipt of major gifts;
- totals for gifts to date from various constituencies, such as the board of directors or alumni;

- launching of area campaigns and their victories;
- special events to boost contributions;
- achievement of significant totals on the way to the goal;
- the victory celebration when the goal is reached; and
- groundbreakings for new buildings.

The publications that support a capital campaign emphasize many of the themes expressed in other public relations strategies. The most important campaign publication is the case statement, which presents an honest appraisal of the institution (its mission and priorities, strengths and weaknesses, its position among peer institutions) and the rationale for support.

A guide for giving, listing methods of making gifts and their advantages, is also an essential piece in the capital campaign.

Important as well is a publication that focuses on the various components for which funds are being sought, and explains how their acquisition will enhance teaching, learning, and research.

Some campaigns need several separate publications to highlight different campaign elements. These are targeted to appeal to specific groups of prospective donors. For example, to encourage gifts from former athletes, you might prepare a brochure featuring plans for the new physical education center to be built with campaign funds.

Many institutions have found helpful a publication combining brief descriptions of outstanding professors and students with their comments on their experiences as teachers and learners at the institution.

A campaign newsletter is an excellent way to provide progress reports to important constituencies and to motivate leaders and volunteers to greater efforts. You or your staff should write the copy; try to gear it for fast reading and give it a spirited tone. Comment on campaign totals, major gifts, and the groups or individuals who are the best solicitors so far. The newsletter might also outline plans to move closer to the goal.

Quality publications are essential to the successful capital campaign. Not only do they transmit information, but they also accent the stature of the institution, the campaign, and the campaign leaders.

If you don't have the capability to produce first-rate publications in-house, you should hire professional help. Funds spent for quality work pay dividends in dollars raised and in enhanced campaign and institution image. If you decide to use outside publications help, be sure to provide careful monitoring and to retain editorial and graphic control.

Your capital campaign public relations programs should be planned and executed with the highest degree of integrity. Pressure to make faster progress toward dollar goals must never be an excuse for dishonest or unfair action by any member of the campaign's professional or volunteer team.

Evaluation

Your campaign public relations plan deserves the same attention from the campaign strategy group as plans for solicitation. Public relations achievements deserve to be recognized alongside dollars raised.

Ultimately, the campaign's top planning group will evaluate the contributions of public relations strategies to the campaign. The primary criterion must be: Did the campaign meet its goal?

A capital campaign, while strenuous and demanding, provides an excellent setting for the growth and development of members of the public relations staff. It is a stretching time, when staff must stand on tiptoe to meet the requirements both of the campaign and of ongoing university events. By doing so, they will develop or increase their energy, enthusiasm, and cooperation. When these carry over into everyday public relations operations, the results will be outstanding.

A capital campaign gives the institution an opportunity to redefine itself to its loyal constituencies and to define itself to others in ways never before possible. Thus, it captures interest, involvement, and support from both old and new friends.

Chapter 21

The Public University Perspective

Royster C. Hedgepeth
Director of Development
University of Illinois Foundation

T en years ago capital campaigns at public universities were anecdotal notes to fund-raising reports. Today they are an integral part of all such reports. Nearly every major public university in the United States is planning for, is engaged in, or has just finished a major capital campaign. The goals for these campaigns (usually in the multi-hundred million dollar range) dwarf figures presented by public universities 10 years earlier. The "sleeping giants" to which Harold Seymour referred in 1966 have indeed awakened, not only in the Midwest, but across the country. (*Designs for Fund-Raising.* New York: McGraw-Hill, 1966.)

In 1975, *Voluntary Support of Education*, published by the Council for Financial Aid to Education (CFAE), reported that for only the second time in 18 years voluntary support of education had decreased from the level of the previous year. CFAE noted that this decrease matched a recession in the national economy. But in that same year, private support of public universities increased 9.6 percent, and of the top 20 institutions listed in the CFAE survey, four were public universities compared to only two in 1965.

In 1985, the CFAE report described a record year of voluntary support for education. The report also said:

> While support to private colleges and universities still leads that to public universities by a 2 to 1 margin, the gap has narrowed remarkably in the last 10 years. Private fundraising activities of public institutions are becoming more and more productive.

CFAE added that over the past 10 years, total voluntary support of public institutions had quadrupled to more than $1.7 billion.

In 1985, seven public universities were in the top 20 in CFAE's report. Corporate support of higher education, which topped that of alumni giving as the single largest source of support for education, was almost evenly split between public and private colleges and universities.

The growth of successful fund raising by public universities may be the single most significant development in American philanthropy in the last 10 years.

Points of correspondence

The philosophical and conceptual dimensions of the capital campaign remain the same whether the campaign is in a public or private college or university. The need to follow sound fund-raising fundamentals remains the same whether a capital campaign is being conducted in a public or private institution.

Colleges and universities use the capital campaign to provide the focus, energy, and intensity necessary to achieve major fund-raising goals. Campaign planners choose the goals carefully and tell their constituents that the achievement of these particular goals will make the most difference in the life of the institution.

The conceptual design of a capital campaign resembles the inverted pyramid so familiar to fund-raising professionals. The campaign begins by focusing on the very few prospective donors and leaders who will make the difference between success and partial success in the undertaking. As the campaign gains momentum, the efforts spread out to ever increasing numbers of prospective donors while target gift values diminish. At its conclusion the campaign should embrace all of an institution's target audiences and provide them with an opportunity to invest in the campaign. In this way, the capital campaign provides a major enhancement to the institution's annual giving efforts.

The goals for a capital campaign are typically nonrepetitive. Schedules are carefully structured and closely followed. And the use of volunteer energy and peer influence is fundamental.

Within this philosophical and conceptual framework, there is very little difference between capital campaigns in the public or private setting. Priorities must be set internally and markets evaluated externally. Plans must be made and time lines established. Prospects must be identified and volunteers recruited. Budgets must be made and staff members trained. And so on it goes.

Differences

Keeping these points of philosophical and conceptual correspondence in mind, consider some key environmental differences that significantly affect the strategy and implementation of the capital campaign in the public university. The environment here includes the complex of factors that influence how events take place. The strategy is the written plan that guides and motivates the action needed to accomplish goals.

Sometimes the environmental factors differ only in degree, but they still have a very real effect on the fund-raising professional in the public university setting. There are four key environmental differences:

- the public setting;
- the decentralized structure of the institution;
- the entrepreneurial nature of the component parts of the institution; and
- the maturity (or, more accurately, the immaturity) of the fund-raising enterprise in the public university setting.

The public setting

The public university is a creature of the state. As such it has both a public mission and a public trust. The public mission is often expressed in such words as "teaching," "research," and "public service," while the public trust stresses a "sound" or "basic" education at the postsecondary level.

As a creature of the state with a public mission and a public trust, the public institution partakes of the egalitarian nature of public education in the United States. This manifests itself in the belief, however imperfectly it may be implemented, that the state must provide an opportunity for education to all those who desire it. Each person's ability, aptitude, and motivation will determine his or her success.

The public university must compete for public funds with the other agencies of the state. The visibility of that competition, coupled with the egalitarian nature of the system, often leads the general public to believe that the public institution does better than other state agencies in the struggle for funds. While the public apparently does not believe that the public college or university is floating in money, most seem to believe that its funding is adequate to fulfill its mission.

Thus, the public setting affects the leadership, the priorities, the statement of the case, and the timing of a capital campaign.

The trustees of a public university play a different role from those in a private institution. They are part of the external political environment that governs the institution. As such the trustees must be concerned with the competition for public funds and with the fulfillment of the institution's public mission and public trust. While the trustees may affirm and indeed support the concept of private giving for a public university, they often do not see their role as being that of voluntary leaders for private gift fund raising. They may even feel that this would be a conflict of interest with their public trusteeship.

Thus, the public institution needs to depoliticize leadership for capital campaign fund raising. Many public institutions create a separate leadership group to provide the power, resources, and contacts necessary for successful campaigning. In this case, it is vital that communication be clear, consistent, and constant between the trustees and the campaign leadership group.

The public setting influences the professional leadership as well as the elected or volunteer leadership. Officials of public universities must give first priority to maintaining effective relationships with the political power base of the state. This political necessity permeates planning and development at all levels, influencing the selection or election of trustees and the administration of various programs to maintain external relationships and alumni contacts.

The public setting also influences campaign priorities and the method by which they are established. The egalitarian nature, the public trust, and the public mission often lead to the attitude that a campaign should include "something for every one." But capital campaigns, by their very nature, are disproportionate in their impact. The development of priorities in a public institution is a difficult and politically laden process that requires great tolerance and understanding from all the participants.

The public setting influences the statement of the case for a capital campaign. The case statement must acknowledge both the contribution of the state and its responsibility for providing the basic dimensions of sound educational programs and facilities. The case statement must make it very clear that the private support resulting from the campaign will not be a substitute for state support, nor will it provide what the state either could or should provide. The judgment calls on this level are difficult and complex.

The case statement should focus on the "margin of excellence." This may be a timeworn phrase, but it is essential in this context. The campaign does not seek support for operations—that is the public responsibility.

The case for the capital campaign in the public university is that of quality. The public university must demonstrate the value that private support would add to the institution and its programs, as well as to the public mission and the public trust.

And finally, the public setting of a capital campaign in the public college or university has a distinct impact on the timing of the campaign. One of the fundamental reasons for a capital campaign is a sense of urgency to accomplish goals. But the public university setting undercuts this sense of urgency. How can we persuade prospective donors that a particular project is needed *today* when there's always the possibility that the state will fund it next year?

Campaign planners must make clear the distinction between the time-driven targets for private gift fund raising and those needs that are part of the normal functioning of the public university and thus are state supported. It's particularly important to articulate the case for "saving time" or "accelerating progress" when bricks-and-mortar projects are part of the capital campaign.

The decentralized structure

The public university is traditionally a highly decentralized organization. The responsibility for internal control and often for the development of budgetary and programmatic strategies typically belongs to the collegiate level or even the departmental level. As power and responsibility flow downward through the organization, each level retains a vested interest in decisions. While these interests are not necessarily adversarial in nature, there is an element of competition. The sheer size of many of the larger multi-campus universities often intensifies the internal competition for funds, programs, and public attention.

The decentralized structure of the public university affects the perceptions of its external audiences and requires special attention to problems of coordination and control. It influences planning, development of priorities, management and use of volunteers, and the actual solicitation process.

In the planning process, the development of a prospective needs list typically starts at the top and works its way down; the potential components for the campaign are generated from the bottom up. This means that the public university typically has more potential targets or needs than can be accomplished in any given campaign period. While the campaign raises the expectations of all component parts of the institution, many of these expectations will not be met. In fact, some components of the institution may find that their priorities are not even included in the campaign.

One reaction to the selection/exclusion process is splintering. Often that division or department that feels its needs are not being adequately met may attempt to develop its own private gift fund-raising program. (This is discussed below under "The entrepreneurial nature.")

The propensity to include something for everyone is compounded in the selection and articulation of campaign priorities. Most of the external publics with whom the public university deals during a capital campaign are accustomed to a control-oriented management structure.

The challenge is for public university campaigners to develop an internal consensus that enables them to present a coherent campaign image to external publics who may be unfamiliar with the way the decentralized university functions. It's better to present priorities in an institutional framework than as a series of seemingly unrelated partial priorities and objectives.

Campaign planners may also need to help external publics differentiate between the institution's annual and capital campaign programs. While the capital campaign program may present a university-wide appearance, it usually operates in parallel with annual giving programs that focus on the various colleges and departments. There is great potential for confusion among both prospects and volunteers.

When planners decide whether to present priorities and objectives as decentralized items or as part of a university-wide program, and how the campaign relates to annual giving, they must also determine how to achieve campaign coordination and control. In the traditional capital campaign, timetables, solicitation schedules, and other activities are under central control. But in the public university, the concept of control is a difficult one to communicate. In fact, "control" is not an idea that is welcomed on the public campus.

The decentralized structure of the public university stresses participation and negotiation. It is not usually supportive of the intense time-bound nature of an effective campaign structure. Therefore, the planning process must include appropriate faculty and staff so that those key people will understand and accept the concepts of control and timetables that are so essential to the campaign.

The structure of the fund-raising organization for the campaign may further aggravate problems of coordination and control. Some public colleges and universities have an independent foundation, while others have a development office under the general university administrative umbrella. There are advantages and disadvantages to both structures.

Because of the decentralization of decision-making in the public university, the senior fund-raising executive and campaign senior staff will spend a disproportionate amount of time negotiating how, when, and where campaign activities will be coordinated.

One of the primary issues to negotiate is who will cultivate and solicit a particular prospect. This is most often a problem with the prospect who is on everyone's list but has no real attachment to any one program. In the decentralized structure of the public university, this prospect may be contacted independently by a variety of people during the cultivation process. The results often reflect only the different orientation of each contact and shed little light on the prospect's particular interests.

When the time comes for a major prospect solicitation, the university must present a coordinated and articulate front. When a presentation is made, the prospect has a right to expect it to be made within the context of clearly defined institutional priorities. This presentation should represent the best opportunity for the university as a whole, and it should have the support of all internal parties.

Multiple contact also occurs in the enlistment of key volunteers. A volunteer may well be asked to participate at several levels of fund raising and for several constituents within the institution. Effective capital campaigning requires that volunteers have a clear understanding of their "job description" and that they understand the scope of the institution's activity. Multiple calls on their time and energy can lead to confusion and frustration. But, again, the decentralized environment makes it difficult to coordinate job descriptions and requests for volunteers' time. Lack of coherent records within the public college or university often aggravates this problem. (This aspect is discussed below under "The maturity.")

The entrepreneurial nature of component parts

Not only is the public university decentralized, the component parts are encouraged to compete with each other both internally and externally for funding. This leads to the third environmental factor—the entrepreneurial nature of the public university.

The fund-raising professional in this entrepreneurial setting must deal with two different kinds of constituent units—those who have real strength, particularly in the grant-seeking area, and those who have no confidence in their ability to generate private support.

The entrepreneurial nature of the public institution forces capital campaigners to spend large amounts of time in building consensus concerning priorities among the components, regardless of their fund-raising experience. While such consensus is not always possible, an optimal level of agreement should be maintained throughout the campaign.

Another entrepreneurial factor that complicates capital campaigning in the public institution is the argument for split funding. It goes as follows: "If we can raise half the money [or a fourth or three-fourths, whatever the case may be], then the state will provide the other half." In unusual circumstances this approach represents a very real opportunity for the capital campaign. For most institutions, however, state funding does not have nearly the capacity to accommodate all such potential projects, and the expectation that it does will almost inevitably meet with disappointment.

Split funding can work as a campaign strategy if the fund-raising professional is assured at the outset that the state will provide support (that is, the state is making a challenge grant). If not, the professional should work for a consensus that funds for the project will be sought either totally from the state or totally from private sources.

Like decentralization, the entrepreneurial spirit affects the politics of the institution. Discussions of state versus private funding should include faculty who are centers of influence and who represent the primary constituencies of the university. Typically, even institutional commitment must be negotiated.

The entrepreneurial nature of the public university also affects the ability to fund the cost of fund raising itself. As the entrepreneurial fund-raising programs grow in the public institution, the flow of undesignated dollars diminishes. This often causes a severe stress on budgetary sources to support the overall fund-raising efforts of a public university.

Perhaps the single most difficult issue currently facing the fund-raising organization in the public university is that of developing a predictable and stable source of funding for its own operations. There seems to be a consensus that funds raised should pay the cost of fund raising, but implementation is a difficult process that is evolving on a case-by-case basis.

And, finally, the entrepreneurial nature of the public institution affects those areas that we call institutional advancement. The components for fund raising, alumni affairs, public relations, government relations, and so forth often see themselves as competitors rather than as team members. Each seeks to establish a system that rewards success in its own independent area while vying for institutional attention and its share of the limited resources.

This internal competition among advancement professionals is in sharp contrast to their counterparts in private institutions where, at least historically, their professional energies are focused on a unified capital campaign effort.

The maturity (or lack thereof) of the fund-raising enterprise

Competition between the various institutional advancement groups is as much a factor of the relative newness of the enterprise in the public university as anything else. Fund raising is relatively new for most public colleges and universities, even those that have been through a successful capital campaign. The interrelationships and the mutual support that come with time and experience have not yet had time to mature.

This lack of coherence is most apparent in those institutions with separate corporations to support fund raising and alumni activities. While organizations supporting alumni activities have an established history in the public university, fund-raising organizations are the new kids on the block. All too often these two organizations see themselves as mutually exclusive, if not directly competitive or even adversarial.

To the outside observer who does not know or care about the differences, the messages may appear redundant, confusing, or even conflicting. The public university can ill afford these differences and the internal competition and duplication of effort that result. As the demands for capital campaigning grow in the public university, the historic differences between alumni activities and fund raising will have to be resolved so that the two organizations can focus clearly on the development of private support for institutional priorities.

Advancement professionals must be convinced that their internal role is to support the emerging fund-raising strength of the institution and its component parts, and their external role is to present a coherent vision of the university. In doing this, they should use the excitement generated by the university and its component parts to develop the interest, involvement, and support of the institution's alumni and friends.

Lack of maturity of advancement programs is perhaps nowhere more evident than in the areas of support services and records management. Many public institutions are within recent memory of the 3 x 5 card as the primary method for tracking alumni and friends. Most public universities are wrestling with fragmented data bases and difficulties of access to those data bases. What the successful private institutions take as a given in planning for a capital campaign is still a novelty for the public university.

The public university must embrace emerging concepts of internal data management, and its decentralized entrepreneurial activities must find sources of administrative support in terms of data management. As the growth of fund-raising programs emulates the decentralized entrepreneurial nature of the public institution, the need for ready access to information is going to be a very high priority. The new technology also brings new problems, such as assuring confidentiality of records and developing an electronic means for maintaining a data base that receives a variety of often disparate input.

For most public institutions the leap from a paper-and-pencil records management system to a complex electronic system is going to be dramatic.

The sheer size of many public universities has a great impact on their record-keeping problems. Most of the nation's largest universities are state supported, and some have over a quarter of a million alumni and friends. Keeping prospect information both current and accessible is a major challenge in itself. The size and population spread of alumni and friends create strategic problems that can endanger the success of the capital campaign.

And finally, and perhaps of greatest importance, because of the relative newness of major fund-raising programs on behalf of public colleges and universities, campaign strategies must be designed to educate both internal and external audiences about the need for private support. The fund-raising program must seize every opportunity to educate alumni, friends, faculty, and staff about the value of private gift fund raising for the public college or university.

The relative newness of the fund-raising enterprise is perhaps the most pervasive of all the environmental factors that make the capital campaign at a public institution different from one in the private sector. As public university fund-raising programs mature, the internal strength that comes from the cooperation of component parts will lead to greater success in capital campaign activities.

Conclusion

Both public and private institutions must adhere to sound, proven fund-raising principles in their capital efforts. But the environment of the institution has a major impact on the strategy developed to achieve fund-raising goals.

The public institution must serve the public trust and give careful priority to those projects defined as the objects of the capital campaign. The decentralized and entrepreneurial character of the public institution mandates an extraordinary degree of negotiation and coordination in pursuit of campaign goals. The need for control must be balanced with the need to preserve the strengths that are inherent in the decentralized, entrepreneurial environment. And the novelty of major campaigning for public universities affects the focus, direction, and implementation of capital campaign activities.

The capital campaign in the public setting is filled with exciting possibilities. The public university's ability to deal with its peculiar environmental factors and to educate its internal and external constituencies will determine whether it can continue—and even intensify—the growth of private gift fund raising that has been established in the past 10 years.

Conclusion

Paul J. Franz, Jr.
Vice President for Development
Lehigh University

What is the future of the capital campaign? With the stock market, you can safely predict that it will go either up or down, but we really can't say what will happen to the capital campaign. Death and taxes seem to have great staying power, and it may well be that capital campaigns will prove just as persistent. Higher education's need for capital funds appears to be a permanent part of our culture. And the need for endowment funds and funds for facilities is definitely on the rise.

The number of capital campaigns has increased in recent years, and goals have reached proportions that only 10 years ago would have seemed astronomical if not preposterous. Today, as Royster Hedgepeth points out in Chapter 21 of this book, even tax-supported institutions are increasingly turning to private sources and the capital campaign to supplement reduced federal and state expenditures for education.

The capital campaign has evolved over a period of time. The components that make it up have been amply described in the chapters of this book. However, while we can be sure that our educational institutions will continue to need capital funds, we can't be sure that the capital campaign will be the method used to obtain them. Many years ago, John D. Millett, former president of Miami University and a noted educator, made a profound statement: "One of the peculiarities of private philanthropy is that effort is needed to obtain it."

A change in method may well be in order, but certainly there can be no pause in the effort to secure capital funds. Many institutions consider it proper strategy to undertake a capital campaign program every eight to 10 years because that's just about how long it takes to finish one campaign and plan the next. These periodic intensive efforts requiring the mobilization of volunteers in record numbers have been aptly referred to as "total war." But in previous years a period of "peace" came after this "war" as the development effort switched back to normal with renewed concentration on the annual fund, planned giving, and other ongoing efforts. This was "the pause that refreshes."

Today, however, for many institutions this familiar pattern no longer exists. The successful completion of a capital campaign brings no lessening of the urgent need for capital funds. Frequently, the work continues in the form of mini-campaigns that tackle the capital needs of one part of the institution, such as an academic department or school within the university. While these mini-campaigns may not possess all the elements of the intensive campaign, the basic techniques are there in some form. And there is no letdown in the effort involved.

The future for capital campaigning looks encouraging no matter what the pessimists may say. The potential in both dollars and volunteers appears to be greater at this moment than at any time in the past.

For years, while we've been warned of the demise of the multi-million dollar gift, these gifts have continued to proliferate. From time to time, tax revisions have cast their pall on the future. But philanthropy has always come through relatively unscathed or, after a brief setback, has gone on to new highs. Then, for a while, it appeared that volunteer leadership was wearing thin. But recently a brand-new leadership has emerged to supplement leaders in their sixties and seventies. For these young graduates, participation in a capital campaign can be just as exciting as it was when their parents made their first solicitation calls.

New technology has also come to our aid. Better software will soon be available along with more standard programs. There will be more information in computer banks about major prospects. Electronic screening may prove useful. Undoubtedly there will be greater use of audio-visuals that can be sent directly to major donors to play on their own VCRs. Other inventions will surely follow.

Perhaps you should discount some of my enthusiasm for the future as due to the incorrigible optimism of the development professional. However, philanthropy, particularly in this country, has become such an important part of our culture that it is difficult, if not impossible, to expect any diminution in the years ahead. As Burr Gibson, chairman of Marts & Lundy, said, "One must assume that the capital campaign will continue to be a part of the long-term strategy of every organization that depends, at least partially, on fund-raising income."